CELEBRATE 2000!
Reflections on the Holy Spirit

Celebrate 2000!

Reflections on the Holy Spirit

POPE JOHN PAUL II

Selected and Arranged by
Paul Thigpen, Ph.D.

CHARIS

Servant Publications
Ann Arbor, Michigan

Charis Books is an imprint of Servant Publications especially designed to serve Roman Catholics.

All selections have been taken from the official Vatican translation of papal documents. Some are from encyclicals and apostolic letters published in the United States by Pauline Books & Media. Other texts appeared originally in the official Vatican newspaper, *L'Osservatore Romano* (English edition, Via del Pellegrino, 00120 Vatican City, Europe). They were reprinted in *The Pope Speaks,* a bimonthly periodical published by *Our Sunday Visitor* (200 Noll Plaza, Huntington, IN 46750). Used by permission. All rights reserved.

Published by Servant Publications
P.O. Box 8617
Ann Arbor, Michigan 48107

Cover photograph: Bettmann Archives. Used by permission.

97 98   99 00 10 9 8 7 6 5 4 3 2 1

Printed in the United States of America
ISBN 1-56955-065-4

LIBRARY OF CONGRESS CATALOGING-IN-PUBLICATION DATA

John Paul II, Pope, 1920 -
 [Selections, English, 1996]
 Celebrate 2000!: reflections on the Holy Spirit: readings for 1998 / Pope John Paul II: selected and arranged by Paul Thigpen.
  p. cm.
 "This book contains the complete text of the apostolic letter, The coming of the third millenium."—CIP galley.
 Includes bibliographical references (p.).
 ISBN 1-56955-065-4
1. Holy Spirit—Meditations. 2. Devotional calendars—Catholic Church.
3. Catholic Church—Prayer-books and devotions—English. 4. Catholic Church—Doctrines—Papal documents. I. Thigpen, Thomas Paul, 1954-
II. Title. III. Series.
BT121.2.J63 1997   97-23169
242'.2—dc21   CIP

Contents

Before We Can Celebrate,
We Have to Meditate

As the new millennium approaches, prophecies of doomsday grow increasingly shrill. Yet in the midst of these troubled and troubling voices, a calmer, more optimistic voice calls out to focus attention on the year 2000. While others cry, "Repent—for the end is near," Pope John Paul II declares, "Repent—for a new beginning has come!" While some prepare for disaster, he calls the Church and indeed the whole world to prepare instead for the third millennium, with a burning hope that God the Father, through Christ and His Spirit, is still at work to renew His beloved creation.

The future, insists the Pope, holds remarkable possibilities for those who open themselves to the Holy Spirit's intentions. The year 2000 is actually a door of divine grace. If we will cross this "threshold of hope" into God's purposes, he says, we can take part in a "new springtime" that heralds the transformation of ourselves, our Church, our nation, and our entire planet.

Confident in this hope, Pope John Paul has announced that the Church will observe the year 2000 as a "Great Jubilee": a particular year of God's favor, a sign of His unfailing love, a season to remember and rejoice that two millennia ago, Christ came to set us free from the bonds of sin. Like all Jubilee years, it will be, he says, "a year of the remission of sins and of the punishments due them, a year of reconciliation between disputing parties, a year of manifold conversions and of ... penance." The Pope wants the entire year to be celebrated exuberantly as an unprecedented birthday party for Jesus—and the whole world is invited to come.

But we can't show up at a birthday party dirty-faced, ragged, and empty-handed. We have to get ourselves ready to honor the Lord and to celebrate His coming. No doubt our heavenly Father loves us as we are, spiritual urchins though we may be. Yet He loves us too much to let us remain as we are. For that reason, the Pope calls us to make preparations.

The whole Christian community should enjoy the Great Jubilee as a feast that will nourish our spirits, put a song in our hearts, and send us out into the world dancing. Before that can happen for most of us, however, we have some work to do. It's time to give our souls a bath, to dress in our spiritual best, and to take in our hands the gift of our will, wrapped in a fervent desire to see Christ's kingdom come.

To help us get ready for this grand party, Pope John Paul outlined a strategy in his Apostolic Letter of November 10, 1994, entitled *Tertio Millennio Adveniente*, "As the Third Millennium Draws Near." There, he noted that the Second Vatican Council, subsequent church synods, holy years, and papal teachings have all played their part in moving the Church toward the Jubilee. But in these last few years of the fading second millennium, the Church needs a specific program of practical initiatives designed to prepare us for the dawning third millennium.

The Holy Father called for special preparations in the years 1997, 1998, and 1999 that are intended to turn the Church's attention to God Himself, to help us grow deeper in our knowledge of Him, our love for Him, our joy in Him. Each of these years he asked to be devoted to reflection on a particular Person within the Holy Trinity: Father, Son, and Holy Spirit.

The order in which he called us to meditate on the three Persons of God in these years reflects, at least in one sense, the order in which we encounter them in human history and in our personal lives. The first year, 1997, was intended to center on God the Son, Jesus Christ—the One whose glorious invasion of history and of our lives first allowed us to encounter God face-to-Face. In 1998, we turn our attention to God the Holy Spirit, Love Himself, the Person sent by Christ to set ablaze the hearts of His disciples and, by their hands, to turn the world upside down. In the Spirit's coming at Pentecost, the Church has encountered God as the One who lives in us and through us.

Finally, in the year 1999, we are to focus on God the Father. The Son of God and the Spirit of God came precisely for this reason: to turn our hearts toward the Father, to restore our friendship with Him, to bring us back to His loving embrace. We will center on Him in this last year because He Himself is our final destination, the One we will encounter at last as the source of all things and the fulfillment of all things.

In each year, Pope John Paul suggests, we should allow our meditation on a Person of the Holy Trinity to lead us to reflect as well on certain related themes. Faith, hope, and love—the three "theological virtues," as they have been called—provide one such set of themes. As we turn our souls toward Christ, we should ponder the meaning of faith in Him. As we look to the Holy Spirit, we should dwell on the meaning of the hope He brings. And as we seek out God the Father, who loved the world into being, we should delve deeply into the meaning of this love.

The Holy Father goes on to note that other themes fall naturally into the focus of meditation for each of the three years. Concerns about ecumenism, for example, easily arise when we begin to think of Christ and of all those who call themselves by His name. Thoughts about the nature of the Church accompany thoughts about the Holy Spirit, who fills and energizes the Church. Reflection on God the Father, who created all people, presses us to consider as well our role in serving the world beyond the Church.

Finally, in his apostolic letter the Pope calls all

Christians to take part in the Jubilee preparations. "Everyone," he urges, "is asked to do as much as possible to ensure that the great challenge of the Year 2000 is not overlooked, for this challenge certainly involves a special grace of the Lord for the Church and for the whole of humanity." This book is an effort to heed that call, to make some small contribution to the Church's preparation for that year of divine favor. For what better way could there be to encourage God's people to nourish themselves on these vital themes than to offer Pope John Paul's own profound reflections as food for thought?

How to Use This Book

The structure of this book, which is a compilation of brief excerpts from the Holy Father's extensive written works, follows his strategy for preparation. As a collection of readings with study questions for the year 1998, it centers on God the Holy Spirit, on the virtue of hope, on Mary as a model of hope, and on associated topics such as the nature of the Church and the Kingdom of God, the gifts of the Spirit, and evangelism.

The goal here, of course, is not simply meditation, but transformation. The Pope has called us to look long and hard at God because to know God truly is to love Him, and to love Him truly is to become like Him.

St. Paul spoke of the process long ago: "We all,... beholding the glory of the Lord, are being changed into his likeness" (2 Cor. 3:18 RSV). St. John promised that "we shall be like [God]" when we "see Him as He is"; and even the hope of seeing Him purifies us (see 1 John 3:2-3). In setting our minds on the Lord during these three years, then, we're bathing and dressing our souls, getting ready for Jesus' grand birthday party, where the gift we bring will be ourselves.

Several important concerns have shaped my choice of study questions. First, because I want to encourage a careful reading of what the Holy Father has said, some questions simply require the reader to go back to the text in order to search out a key thought he has made explicit. Other questions, however, point beyond the text to the ideas implicit there—to the critical assumptions or the definitions of significant terms that form the foundation for the meaning of the text.

I've decided, after some deliberation, to pose most of the questions in the first person singular. That is to say, instead of asking the reader, "What does this mean to you and what must you do about it?" this study guide has each person ask him or herself: "What does this mean to *me* and what must *I* do about it?" Such an approach, I think, presses the reader to respond in some personal, immediate way to what the Holy Father has said.

Why not the first person plural—"we" instead of

"I"? No doubt the frequent occurrence of "I" and "me" in the questions could be mistaken as a kind of narrowness or self-centeredness, a neglect of the "we." Yet in many cases *we* cannot get very far in making a difference in the world if there hasn't first been a change in *me*.

The questions here reflect a mix of the theoretical and the practical, the theological and the pastoral, but the emphasis is decidedly on the practical and pastoral. Repeatedly the reader is urged to consider the specific, concrete ways in which he or she can act on the Holy Father's insights. What good, for example, does it accomplish to meditate on the Church's role as a "sacrament of reconciliation" if I don't go on to identify and approach those individuals in my life with whom I need to be reconciled?

Finally, readers will note soon enough that the purpose of these questions is not to challenge the Holy Father, to submit him to a critique, or to provide opportunity for a Church-wide referendum on what he has to say. He already has more than enough critics who busy themselves with such work. These meditations were of course not issued as infallible papal pronouncements, so Catholics aren't under any obligation to agree with them all. Nevertheless, I've chosen precisely these particular excerpts from the vast body of his writings because I'm convinced that in them he forcefully challenges *us* and submits *our* lives to a piercing critique. We can ignore what he has to say only at great peril to ourselves, to the Church, and to the world.

Despite that peril, I place my hope firmly in the Holy Spirit, "the guardian of hope," to open our ears and our hearts. With the Holy Father himself, we can look eagerly to the new millennium—and celebrate with confidence the coming "springtime for the Gospel."

Paul Thigpen

Personal Reflection Questions

THE HOLY SPIRIT OF GOD

1. The Spirit of Holiness
   * Why do I need the Holy Spirit to become holy myself?
   * What shape must holiness take in the particular circumstances of my life?

2. The Holy Spirit, Uncreated Gift
   * In what current situations do I feel close to despair and thus have the greatest need for the Holy Spirit to become my "guardian of hope"?
   * If the Holy Spirit "convinces concerning sin," what sins might He be bringing to my attention "in order to restore what is good" in me?

3. The Holy Spirit, Help of the Church
   * In what ways have I personally experienced joy to be "the fruit of love, and therefore of God who is love"?
   * How does the happiness "which only in God has its complete realization" differ from other kinds of happiness I have sought—perhaps in vain?

4. The Fruit of the Spirit
   * What specific virtues do I most need to cultivate through submission to "the saving action of the Holy Spirit"?

- What does it mean "to set the mind on the Spirit"?

5. The Holy Spirit and Prayer
   - How does prayer become "the voice of all those who apparently have no voice"?
   - In the times when I "do not know how to pray" as I ought, how might I allow the Spirit to guide my prayer "from within"?

6. "Receive the Holy Spirit!"
   - How might I begin to "share in the eternity of God Himself," in the "divine life," even now?
   - What kind of inheritance—both privileges and responsibilities—accompanies my adoption as a son or daughter of God?

THE VIRTUE OF HOPE

7. Hope for the Third Millennium
   - Hope, along with faith and love, is considered a "theological virtue"—that is, a virtue whose goal and motive is God. How does hope motivate us to draw close to God?
   - When am I most tempted to "lose sight of the final goal which gives meaning and value to life"?

8. Signs of Hope
   - What "signs of hope" in my personal life, my parish and my community have I tended to overlook?

- How could I become a "sign of hope" to those around me?

9. The Holy Spirit, Guardian of Hope
   - In what practical ways can I join the Spirit and the Church in inviting Jesus to "Come!" each day?
   - What circumstances in the Church today call for us to "persevere in hope" despite discouragement and disappointment?

10. Spiritual Hunger Is a Sign of Hope
    - What signs of "spiritual hunger" do I see in those around me?
    - What kinds of spiritual "food" can I offer to those who are hungry for it?

11. Renewal of Prayer Is a Sign of Hope
    - Have I allowed the great challenges of "our difficult age" to drive me deeper into prayer?
    - How might I pray with and for the individuals I know who are in danger of losing hope because of adversity?

12. A New Springtime for the Gospel
    - Has pessimism about the world's future dampened my desire to share the Gospel?
    - When I move in non-Christian circles, do I look for "Gospel ideals and values" that I can affirm and encourage?

MARY, MODEL OF HOPE

13. Mary, Woman of Hope
    - How might I imitate Mary in both "silence and attentiveness" in the presence of God?
    - To what specific "promises of God" might I entrust myself as Mary did?

14. Mary, Hope in Our Struggle With Sin
    - How does Mary serve as "the unchangeable and inviolable sign of God's election"—a sign of hope that He has chosen us for a destiny with Him?
    - In which particular "struggles with sin" do I most need the help of the Blessed Mother's intercession and the Spirit's grace?

15. Mary, Sign of Sure Hope
    - Do I see the "deserts" of my life not only as "places of trial" but also as places of "the manifestation of God's love" for me?
    - How might I, like the Virgin Mother, cultivate in my daily life a "certainty that God is near" me and caring for me despite adversity?

THE CHURCH

16. Christ Comes to the Church Through the Holy Spirit
    - Why was Jesus' return to the Father in heaven not an abandonment of His people?
    - How does Christ come to us in the sacraments

of the Church through the power of the Holy Spirit?

17. The Church, Great Sacrament of Reconciliation
    • What does it mean for the Church to be the "sacrament of reconciliation" for the world?
    • How can I help make sure my parish is "a reconciled community which witnesses to and represents in the world the work of Christ"?

18. The Church's Work of Reconciliation
    • How can I take part in the Church's "prophetic mission" to "condemn the evil of sin, to proclaim the need for conversion, to invite and ask people to let themselves be reconciled" to God?
    • Are there any individuals with whom I need to be reconciled by seeking mutual understanding or forgiveness?

19. The Church's Witness to Moral Truth
    • How is the Church's firm defense of God's universal and eternal moral truths an expression of love for the world?
    • On what moral issues have I been tempted to avoid taking a clear stand because the position I hold as a Christian is unpopular or controversial?

20. The Meaning of the Kingdom of God
    • Why do visions of "the Kingdom of God" that are merely political, social, economic, or

cultural prove in the end to be incomplete
and even dangerous?
- Why is our appreciation of the "mystery of
creation" inadequate if we fail to take into
consideration creation's need for the "mystery of redemption"?

21. The Kingdom of God Is a Person
- Why can the true "Kingdom of God" never
be detached from Christ and His Church?
- What "specific and necessary role" is conferred on the Church by her unique relationship with Christ and the Spirit?

22. The Importance of the Parish
- What indispensable role is played by the local
parish within the mission of the universal
Church?
- In what practical ways can I help make my
parish "a house of welcome to all and a place
of service to all"?

23. The Church Needs Ongoing Conversion
- In what specific areas of my life do I need to
"purify and renew" myself as part of my
"ongoing conversion"?
- What are the "ultimate questions" that trouble people whose answers can be found "only
in Christ"?

THE SACRAMENTS

24. The Holy Spirit and the Sacraments
    • How does the Holy Spirit "strengthen the inner man" through the Eucharist?
    • In what ways do the other sacraments bring us grace and life?

25. The Eucharist, Center and Summit of Sacramental Life
    • Why does "the entire sacramental life of the Church" reach its "center and summit" in the Eucharist?
    • Does my attitude toward the Eucharist reflect an appreciation of this reality?

26. The Church Lives by the Eucharist
    • Why must the Eucharist never be treated merely as an occasion for manifesting the human brotherhood of Christ's disciples?
    • What does it mean for the Eucharist to be "at one and the same time a Sacrifice-sacrament, a Communion-sacrament, and a Presence-sacrament"?

27. The Eucharist and the Kingdom
    • Why is the bond of the Eucharist "stronger than any natural union"?
    • How does the Kingdom of God become present in the celebration of the Eucharist?

28. Eucharistic Worship Leads to Charity
    - Why is the Eucharist called "the Sacrament of Love"?
    - When I receive the Eucharist, how might I learn to "consciously share" in the love that it signifies and inspires?

29. The Eucharist, School of Love
    - How does the Eucharist teach us "what value … each person has in God's eyes"?
    - How can the Eucharist make us "sensitive to all human suffering and misery, to all injustice and wrong," and inspire us to seek a remedy for these problems?

UNITY IN THE CHURCH

30. Catholic Unity
    - Why is every Catholic responsible to work for the unity of the Church?
    - Why is "ecclesial obedience" necessary for unity in the Church?

31. A Credible Sign of Reconciliation
    - How have divisions in the Church become a source of scandal to a watching world?
    - In what ways may I have sometimes contributed to "polarization and destructive criticism … in the household of faith"?

32. The Mystery of Communion
    - Why must the communion of Christians have its source in their communion with Christ?

- How can I employ my particular combination of "ministries and charisms" in a way that complements those of others in my parish?

33. We Cannot Remain in Isolation
   - In what ways am I sometimes tempted to isolate myself from the life of the Church?
   - When I see the differences in "capacity for service" among the members of my parish, do I nevertheless recognize an "equal dignity" in them all?

34. Paths to Unity in the Church
   - In what ways have we failed to "relinquish our own subjective views and seek the truth where it is to be found" in the Scripture and its authentic interpretation by the Magisterium of the Church?
   - Do I ever subordinate the clear teaching of the Church to my own "opinions, fashions, and ideological choices"?

35. Unity Is the Fruit of Conversion
   - How does unity spring from "sincere acceptance of the unchanging principles laid down by Christ for His Church"?
   - Why is an "effective communion" with the Holy Father, the "successor of Peter," necessary for every person who wishes to remain Catholic and be recognized as Catholic?

CLERGY, RELIGIOUS, AND LAITY

36. A Diversity of Gifts
    - In what specific ways does the lay state of life recall for priests and religious the "significance of the earthly and temporal realities in the [saving] plan of God"?
    - To what realities do the ministerial priesthood and the religious state bear witness?

37. Pray and Work for Vocations
    - How might I find ways to "pray and work tirelessly" for vocations in my family and my parish?
    - Am I open to the possibility that God may have a vocation in mind for me or for my children?

38. The Clergy: A Grace for the Whole Church
    - How is the participation in Christ's priesthood that is given to the ordained ministers different "not simply in degree but in essence" from the participation given to all the lay faithful through Baptism and Confirmation?
    - How might pastors "acknowledge and foster the ministries, the offices, and roles of the lay faithful"?

39. Priests Represent Christ
    - What does the Holy Spirit accomplish through the Sacrament of Orders?

- In what ways do priests serve as a "sacramental representation of Jesus Christ"?

40. On the Shortage of Priests
    - Why can the problems caused by a shortage of priests be "alleviated only secondarily or temporarily by having lay people in some way supply for them"?
    - Why is there danger in "clericalizing the lay faithful or ... laicizing priests"?

41. Priests Will Continue to the End of Time
    - What is the "essential aspect of the priest that does not change"?
    - Why is the priesthood "destined to last in endless succession throughout history"?

42. The Lay Faithful: Called to Holiness
    - What is the "prime and fundamental vocation" of every lay person?
    - In what practical ways is this vocation fulfilled in a "life according to the Spirit"?

43. The Charisms of the Holy Spirit
    - Toward what goal must the exercise of the Spirit's charisms be directed?
    - Why is the "discernment of charisms" always necessary?

44. Lay Participation and Cooperation in Church Affairs
    - Why is it an error to "judge ecclesial structures of participation and cooperation by secular democratic standards"?

- How might pastors be attentive to the ideas of the lay faithful while still exercising the freedom and authority that God has given them as shepherds of His people?

EVANGELIZATION AND MISSION

45. The Urgency of Missionary Activity
    - What specific "difficulties both internal and external have weakened the Church's missionary thrust toward non-Christians"?
    - Why is missionary evangelization the "primary service" that the Chuch can render to the world?

46. New Opportunities for Evangelization
    - What new opportunities worldwide have opened doors to evangelization?
    - Do these new circumstances present any concrete opportunities for proclaiming Christ in my tiny corner of the world?

47. Lay Holiness and Lay Mission
    - How can I bring the truths of the Gospel to bear in concrete ways on my involvement in temporal affairs?
    - Why must my personal mission and ministry be built on a foundation of personal holiness?

48. Sharers in Christ's Mission
    - In what practical ways can I take part in Christ's priestly, prophetic, and kingly missions in my parish?

- In what ways might I work to help "restore to ... all its original value" that portion of God's creation for which I have primary responsibility?

49. Evangelization Is the Task of Every Christian
    - Why is it that "faith is strengthened and grows precisely when it is given to others"?
    - Do I know anyone "caught by the mechanisms of secularism and indifference" with whom I might share "the gift of salvation"?

50. Proclaiming Christ
    - Why is a "silent witness" necessary but not enough to fulfill my mission of proclaiming Christ?
    - Considering my own circle of witness and influence, what are the particular "places and circumstances where [I] alone can bring the seed of God's word"?

51. Witness, the First Form of Evangelization
    - Why do people "put more trust in witnesses than in teachers, in experience than in teaching, and in life and action than in theories"?
    - How might I practice bearing "the witness of humility"?

52. A New Missionary Advent
    - Why has the number of those "awaiting Christ" increased so sharply in recent years?
    - Why must the missionary task "remain foremost" among the endeavors both of the Church as a whole and of every individual believer?

1998

Weekly Readings on
God the Holy Spirit

THE HOLY SPIRIT OF GOD

We turn from our reflections in the first year on God the Son in order to ponder in the second year the mystery of God the Holy Spirit, "the uncreated Gift" sent by the Son to fill the Church with His power.

<u>THE WEEK OF JANUARY 4, 1998</u>

1. THE SPIRIT OF HOLINESS

[Jesus says,] "The Spirit of the Lord is upon me" (Lk 4:18). The Spirit is not simply upon the Messiah, but He fills Him, penetrating every part of Him and reaching to the very depths of all that He is and does. Indeed, the Spirit is the principle of the consecration and mission of the Messiah: "Because he has anointed me and sent me to preach good news to the poor" (see Luke 4:18). Through the Spirit, Jesus belongs totally and exclusively to God and shares in the infinite holiness of God, who calls Him, chooses Him, and sends Him forth. In this way the Spirit of the Lord is revealed as the source of holiness and of the call of holiness.

This same "Spirit of the Lord" is upon the entire people of God, which becomes established as a people consecrated to God and sent by God to announce the Gospel of salvation. The members of the People of God are "inebriated" and "sealed" with the Spirit (see 1 Corinthians 12:13; 2 Corinthians 1:21ff; Ephesians 1:13; 4:30) and called to holiness.

In particular, the Spirit reveals to us and communicates the fundamental calling which the Father addresses to everyone from all eternity: the vocation to be "holy and blameless before him...in love," by virtue of our predestination to be His adopted children through Jesus Christ (Eph 1:4-5). This is not all. By revealing and communicating this vocation to us, the Spirit becomes within us the principle and wellspring of its fulfillment. He, the Spirit of the Son (see Galatians 4:6), configures us to Christ Jesus and makes us sharers in His life as Son—that is, sharers in His life of love for the Father and for our brothers and sisters.

"If we live by the Spirit, let us also walk by the Spirit" (Gal 5:25). In these words the Apostle Paul reminds us that a Christian life is a spiritual life, that is, a life enlivened and led by the Spirit toward holiness or the perfection of charity. [PDV n. 19]

THE WEEK OF JANUARY 11, 1998

2. THE HOLY SPIRIT, UNCREATED GIFT

The Holy Spirit does not cease to be the guardian of hope in the human heart: the hope of all human creatures, and especially of those who "have the first fruits of the Spirit" and "wait for the redemption of their bodies" (see Romans 8:23).

The Holy Spirit, in His mysterious bond of divine communion with the Redeemer of man, is the One who brings about the continuity of His work. He takes from Christ and transmits to all, unceasingly entering into the history of the world through the heart of man. Here He becomes—as the liturgical Sequence of the Solemnity of Pentecost proclaims—the true "father of the poor, giver of gifts, light of hearts."

He becomes the "sweet guest of the soul," whom the Church unceasingly greets on the threshold of the inmost sanctuary of every human being. For He brings rest and relief in the midst of toil, in the midst of the work of human hands and minds. He brings rest and ease in the midst of the heat of the day, in the midst of the anxieties, struggles, and perils of every age. He brings consolation, when the human heart grieves and is tempted to despair. And therefore the same Sequence exclaims: "without your aid nothing is in man, nothing is without fault." For only the Holy Spirit "convinces concerning sin" (see John 16:8), concerning evil, in order to restore what is good in man and in the world: in order to "renew the face of the earth" (Ps 104:30). Therefore, He purifies from everything that disfigures man, from what is unclean. He heals even the deepest wounds of human existence. He changes the interior dryness of souls, transforming them into the fertile fields of grace and holiness. What is hard He softens, what is frozen He warms, what is wayward He sets anew on the paths of salvation.

Praying thus, the Church unceasingly professes her faith that there exists in our created world a Spirit who is an uncreated gift. He is the Spirit of the Father and of the Son: like the Father and the Son He is uncreated, without limit, eternal, omnipotent, God, Lord. This Spirit of God fills the universe, and all that is created recognizes in Him the source of its own identity, finds in Him its own transcendent expression, turns to Him and awaits Him, invokes Him with its own being. Man turns to Him,... the Spirit of truth and of love, man who lives by truth and by love, and who without the source of truth and love cannot live. [DV n. 67]

3. THE HOLY SPIRIT, HELP OF THE CHURCH

To [the Holy Spirit] turns the Church, which is the heart of humanity, to implore for all and dispense to all those gifts of the love which through Him "has been poured into our hearts" (Rom 5:5). To Him turns the Church, along the intricate paths of man's pilgrimage on earth: she implores, she unceasingly implores uprightness of human acts, as the Spirit's work. She implores the joy and consolation that only He, the true Counselor, can bring by coming down into people's inmost hearts. The Church implores the grace of the virtues that merit heavenly glory, implores eternal salvation, in the full communication of the divine life, to which the Father has eternally "predestined" human beings, created through love in the image and likeness of the Most Holy Trinity.

The Church with her heart which embraces all human hearts implores from the Holy Spirit that happiness which only in God has its complete realization: the joy that no one will be able to take away (see John 16:22), the joy which is the fruit of love, and therefore of God who is love. She implores "the righteousness, the peace, and the joy of the Holy Spirit" in which, in the words of St. Paul, consists the Kingdom of God (see Romans 14:17, Galatians 5:22). [DV n. 67]

4. THE FRUIT OF THE SPIRIT

The history of salvation shows that God's coming close and making Himself present to man and the world—that marvelous "condescension" of the Spirit—meets with resistance and opposition in our human reality.... It is St. Paul who describes in a particularly eloquent way the tension and struggle that trouble the human heart. We read in the Letter to the Galatians: "But I say, walk by the Spirit, and do not gratify the desires of the flesh. For the desires of the flesh are against the Spirit, and the desires of the Spirit are against the flesh; for these are opposed to each other, to prevent you from doing what you would" (Gal 5:16-17).

There already exists in man, as a being made up of body and spirit, a certain tension, a certain struggle of tendencies between the "spirit" and the "flesh." But this struggle in fact belongs to the heritage of sin, is a consequence of sin and at the same time a confirmation of it. This is part of everyday experience. As the Apostle writes: "Now the works of the flesh are plain: fornication, impurity, licentiousness... drunkenness, carousing and the like." These are the sins that could be called "carnal." But he also adds others: "enmity, strife, jealousy, anger, selfishness, dissension, party spirit, envy" (see Galatians 5:19-21). All of this constitutes the "works of the flesh."

But with these works, which are undoubtedly evil, Paul contrasts "the fruit of the Spirit," such as "love, joy, peace, patience, kindness, goodness, faithfulness, gentleness, self-control" (Gal 5:22-23). From the context it is clear that for the Apostle it is not a question of discriminating against and condemning the body, with which the spiritual soul constitutes man's nature.... Rather, he is concerned with the morally

good or bad works, or better, the permanent disposi-
tions—virtues and vices—which are the fruit of submission to (in the first case) or of resistance to (in
the second case) the saving action of the Holy Spirit.
Consequently the Apostle writes: "If we live by the
Spirit, let us also walk by the Spirit" (Gal 5:25)....

The contrast that St. Paul makes between life
"according to the Spirit" and life "according to the
flesh" (see Romans 8:5, 9) gives rise to a further contrast: that between life and death. "To set the mind
on the flesh is death, but to set the mind on the
Spirit is life and peace"; hence the warning: "For if
you live according to the flesh you will die, but if by
the Spirit you put to death the deeds of the body
you will live" (Rom 8:6, 13, RSV). Properly understood, this is an exhortation to live in the truth, that
is, according to the dictates of an upright conscience, and at the same time it is a profession of
faith in the Spirit of truth as the One who gives life.
[DV n. 55]

5. THE HOLY SPIRIT AND PRAYER

The breath of the divine life, the Holy Spirit, in its
simplest and most common manner, expresses itself
and makes itself felt in prayer. It is a beautiful and
salutary thought that, wherever people are praying
in the world, there the Holy Spirit is, the living
breath of prayer. It is a beautiful and salutary
thought to recognize that—if prayer is offered
throughout the world, in the past, in the present,
and in the future—equally widespread is the presence and action of the Holy Spirit, who "breathes"

prayer in the heart of man in all the endless range of the most varied situations and conditions, sometimes favorable and sometimes unfavorable to the spiritual and religious life.

Many times, through the influence of the Spirit, prayer rises from the human heart in spite of prohibitions and persecutions and even official proclamations regarding the nonreligious or even atheistic character of public life. Prayer always remains the voice of all those who apparently have no voice—and in this voice there always echoes that "loud cry" attributed to Christ by the Letter to the Hebrews (see Hebrews 5:7).

Prayer is also the revelation of that abyss which is the heart of man: a depth which comes from God and which only God can fill, precisely with the Holy Spirit. We read in Luke: "If you, then, who are evil, know how to give good gifts to your children, how much more will the heavenly Father give the Holy Spirit to those who ask him" (Lk 11:13).

The Holy Spirit is the gift that comes into man's heart together with prayer. In prayer He manifests Himself first of all and above all as the gift that "helps us in our weakness" (Rom 8:26). This is the magnificent thought developed by St. Paul in the Letter to the Romans, when he writes: "For we do not know how to pray as we ought, but the Spirit himself intercedes for us with sighs too deep for words" (Rom 8:26).

Therefore, the Holy Spirit not only enables us to pray, but guides us from within in prayer: He is present in our prayer and gives it a divine dimension. Thus "he who searches the hearts of men knows what is the mind of the Spirit, because the Spirit intercedes for the saints according to the will of God" (Rom 8:27). Prayer through the power of the Holy Spirit becomes the evermore mature expression of the new man, who by means of this prayer participates in the divine life. [DV n. 65]

6. "RECEIVE THE HOLY SPIRIT!"

The whole person, body and soul, is destined to eternal life. And eternal life is life in God. Not life in the world, which, as St. Paul teaches, is "subjected to futility" (Rom 8:20). As a creature in the world, the individual is subject to death, just like every other created being. The immortality of the whole person can come only as a gift from God. It is in fact a sharing in the eternity of God Himself.

How do we receive this life in God? Through the Holy Spirit! Only the Holy Spirit can give this new life, as we profess in the Creed: "I believe in the Holy Spirit, the Lord, the giver of life." Through Him we become, in the likeness of the only-begotten Son, adopted children of the Father.

When Jesus says, "Receive the Holy Spirit!" (Jn 20:22) He is saying: Receive from Me this divine life, the divine adoption which I brought into the world and which I grafted on to human history. I myself, the Eternal Son of God, through the power of the Holy Spirit, became the Son of Man, born of the Virgin Mary. You, through the power of the same Spirit, must become—in Me and through Me— adopted sons and daughters of God.

"Receive the Holy Spirit!" means: Accept from Me

this inheritance of grace and truth, which makes you one spiritual and mystical body with Me. "Receive the Holy Spirit!" also means: Become sharers in the Kingdom of God, which the Holy Spirit pours into your hearts as the fruit of the suffering and sacrifice of the Son of God, so that more and more God will become all in all (see 1 Corinthians 15:28). [TPS 40/3, 1995, 164-5]

THE VIRTUE OF HOPE

It is "by the power of the Holy Spirit," the Apostle Paul says, that we are able to "abound in hope." His comforting pres ence today encourages us to place our tomorrow in the hands of "the God of hope" who loves us (Rom 15:13).

THE WEEK OF FEBRUARY 15, 1998

7. HOPE FOR THE THIRD MILLENNIUM

Believers should be called to a renewed appreciation of the theological virtue of hope, which they have already heard proclaimed "in the word of the truth, the Gospel" (Col 1:5). The basic attitude of hope, on the one hand, encourages the Christian not to lose sight of the final goal which gives meaning and value to life; and on the other, [it] offers solid and profound reasons for a daily commitment to God's plan.

As the Apostle Paul reminds us: "We know that the whole creation has been groaning in travail together until now; and not only the creation, but we ourselves, who have the first fruits of the Spirit, groan inwardly as we wait for adoption as sons, the redemption of our bodies. For in this hope we were saved"

(Rom 8:22-24). Christians are called to prepare for the Great Jubilee of the beginning of the third millennium by renewing their hope in the definitive coming of the Kingdom of God, preparing for it daily in their hearts, in the Christian community to which they belong, in their particular social context, and in world history itself. [TMA n. 46]

8. SIGNS OF HOPE

There is... a need for a better appreciation and understanding of the signs of hope present in the last part of this century, even though they often remain hidden from our eyes. In society in general, such signs of hope include scientific, technological, and especially medical progress in the service of human life; a greater awareness of our responsibility for the environment; efforts to restore peace and justice wherever they have been violated; a desire for reconciliation and solidarity among different peoples, particularly in the complex relationship between the north and the south of the world.

In the Church, [signs of hope] include a greater attention to the voice of the Spirit through the acceptance of charisms and the promotion of the laity; a deeper commitment to the cause of Christian unity; and the increased interest in dialogue with other religions and with contemporary culture. [TMA n. 46]

9. THE HOLY SPIRIT, GUARDIAN OF HOPE

The Church, united with the Virgin Mother, prays unceasingly as the Bride to her divine Spouse, as the words of the Book of Revelation.... attest: "The Spirit and the bride say to the Lord Jesus Christ: Come!" (see Revelation 22:17). The Church's prayer is this unceasing invocation, in which "the Spirit himself intercedes for us" (Rom 8:26). In a certain sense, the Spirit Himself utters it *with* the Church and *in* the Church.

For the Spirit is given to the Church in order that through His power the whole community of the People of God, however widely scattered and diverse, may persevere in hope: that hope in which "we have been saved" (see Romans 8:24). It is... the hope of definitive fulfillment in God, the hope of the eternal Kingdom, that is brought about by participation in the life of the Trinity. The Holy Spirit, given to the Apostles as the Counselor, is the guardian and animator of this hope in the heart of the Church. [DV n. 66]

10. SPIRITUAL HUNGER IS A SIGN OF HOPE

Our times are both momentous and fascinating. While on the one hand people seem to be pursuing material prosperity and to be sinking ever deeper into consumerism and materialism, on the other hand we are witnessing a desperate search for meaning, the need for an inner life, and a desire to learn new forms and methods of meditation and prayer. Not only in cultures with strong religious elements, but also in secularized societies, the spiritual dimension of life is being sought after as an antidote to dehumanization.

This phenomenon—the so-called "religious revival"—is not without ambiguity, but it also represents an opportunity. The Church has an immense spiritual patrimony to offer humankind, a heritage in Christ, who called Himself "the way, and the truth, and the life" (Jn 14:6): It is the Christian path to meeting God, to prayer, to asceticism, and to the search for life's meaning. [RM n. 38]

11. RENEWAL OF PRAYER IS A SIGN OF HOPE

Our difficult age has a special need of prayer. In the course of history—both in the past and in the present—many men and women have borne witness to the importance of prayer by consecrating themselves to the praise of God and to the life of prayer, especially in monasteries and convents. So, too, recent years have been seeing a growth in the number of people who, in evermore widespread movements and groups, are giving first place to prayer and seeking in prayer a renewal of their spiritual life. This is a significant and comforting sign, for from this experience there is coming a real contribution to the revival of prayer among the faithful, who have been helped to gain a clearer idea of the Holy Spirit as He who inspires in hearts a profound yearning for holiness.

In many individuals and many communities there is a growing awareness that, even with all the rapid progress of technological and scientific civilization, and despite the real conquests and goals attained, man is threatened, humanity is threatened. In the face of this danger, and indeed already experiencing the frightful reality of man's spiritual decadence, individuals and whole communities, guided as it were by an inner sense of faith, are seeking the strength to raise man up again, to save him from himself, from his own errors and mistakes that often make harmful his very conquests. And thus they are discovering prayer, in which the "Spirit who helps us in our weakness" manifests Himself. In this way the times in which we are living are bringing the Holy Spirit closer to the many who are returning to prayer. [DV n. 65]

12. A NEW SPRINGTIME FOR THE GOSPEL

If we look at today's world, we are struck by many negative factors that can lead to pessimism. But this feeling is unjustified: we have faith in God our Father and Lord, in His goodness and mercy. As the third millennium of the Redemption draws near, God is preparing a great springtime for Christianity, and we can already see its first signs. In fact, both in the non-Christian world and in the traditionally Christian world, people are gradually drawing closer to Gospel ideals and values, a development which the Church seeks to encourage. Today in fact there is a new consensus among peoples about these values: the rejection of violence and war; respect for the human person and for human rights; the desire for freedom, justice, and brotherhood; the surmounting of different forms of racism and nationalism; the affirmation of the dignity and role of women.

Christian hope sustains us in committing ourselves fully to the new evangelization and to the worldwide mission, and leads us to pray as Jesus taught us: "Thy kingdom come. Thy will be done, on earth as it is in heaven" (Mt 6:10).

MARY, MODEL OF HOPE

Our Lord's Mother lived her life in the firm hope that God's promises to her would be fulfilled; she has become for us the Mother of hope.

THE WEEK OF MARCH 29, 1998

13. MARY, WOMAN OF HOPE

Mary, who conceived the Incarnate Word by the power of the Holy Spirit—and then in the whole of her life allowed herself to be guided by His interior activity—will be contemplated and imitated during this year above all as the woman who was docile to the voice of the Spirit, a woman of silence and attentiveness, a woman of hope who, like Abraham, accepted God's will "hoping against hope" (see Romans 4:18). Mary gave full expression to the longing of the poor of Yahweh and is a radiant model for those who entrust themselves with all their hearts to the promises of God. [TMA n. 48]

THE WEEK OF APRIL 5, 1998

14. MARY, HOPE IN OUR STRUGGLE WITH SIN

In the [saving] design of the Most Holy Trinity, the mystery of the Incarnation constitutes the superabundant fulfillment of the promise made by God to man after original sin, after that first sin whose effects oppress the whole earthly history of man (see Genesis 3:15). And so, there comes into the world a Son, "the seed of the woman" who will crush the evil of sin in its very origins: "he will crush the head of the serpent."...The victory of the woman's Son will not take place without a hard struggle, a struggle that is to extend through the whole of human history....

Mary, Mother of the Incarnate Word, is placed at the very center of that... struggle which accompanies the history of humanity on earth and the history of salvation itself. In this central place, she who belongs to the weak and poor of the Lord (see Luke 1:46-55) bears in herself, like no other member of the human race, that glory of grace which the Father has bestowed on us in His Beloved Son, and this grace determines the extraordinary greatness and beauty of her whole being. Mary thus remains before God, and also before the whole of humanity, as the unchangeable and inviolable sign of God's election, spoken of in Paul's letter: "in Christ... he chose us... before the foundation of the world... he destined us... to be his sons" (Eph 1:4-5].

This election is more powerful than any experience of evil and sin... which marks the history of man. In this history Mary remains a sure sign of hope. [RMa n. 11]

15. MARY, SIGN OF SURE HOPE

The angel's Annunciation to Mary is framed by these reassuring words: "Do not be afraid, Mary," and, "With God nothing will be impossible" (Lk 1:30, 37.

The whole of the Virgin Mother's life is in fact pervaded by the certainty that God is near to her and that He accompanies her with His providential care.

The same is true of the Church, which finds "a place prepared by God" (Rv 12:6) in the desert, the place of trial but also of the manifestation of God's love for his people (see Hosea 2:16). Mary is a living word of comfort for the Church in her struggle against death. Showing us the Son, the Church assures us that in Him the forces of death have already been defeated: "Death with life contended: combat strangely ended! Life's own Champion, slain, yet lives to reign."[1]

The Lamb who was slain is alive, bearing the marks of His Passion in the splendor of the Resurrection. He alone is master of all the events of history: He opens its "seals" (see Revelation 5:1-10) and proclaims, in time and beyond, the power of life over death. In the new Jerusalem, that new world toward which human history is traveling, "death shall be no more, neither shall there be mourning nor crying nor pain any more, for the former things have passed away" (Rv 21:4, RSV).

And as we, the pilgrim people, the people of life and for life, make our way in confidence toward a "new heaven and a new earth" (Rv 21:1), we look to her who is for us "a sign of sure hope and solace."[2] [EV n. 105]

THE CHURCH

The Church was born on the day of Pentecost, when the Spirit came upon Christ's followers; the Spirit is the One who empowers the Church to be a sacrament of Christ's life in the world.

16. CHRIST COMES TO THE CHURCH THROUGH THE HOLY SPIRIT

As the end of the second Millennium approaches—an event which should recall to everyone and as it were make present anew the coming of the Word [that is, Christ] in the fullness of time—the Church once more means to ponder the very essence of her divine-human constitution and of that mission which enables her to share in the messianic mission of Christ.... Following this line, we can go back to the Upper Room, where Jesus Christ reveals the Holy Spirit as the Paraclete [Advocate], the Spirit of truth, and where He speaks of His own departure through the Cross as the necessary condition for the Spirit's coming: "It is to your advantage that I go away, for if I do not go away, the Counselor will not come to you; but if I go, I will send him to you" (Jn 16:7).... This prediction first came true the evening of Easter day and then during the celebration of Pentecost in Jerusalem, and... ever since then it is being fulfilled in human history through the Church.

In the light of that prediction, we also grasp the full meaning of what Jesus says, also at the Last

Supper, about His new coming. For it is significant that in the same farewell discourse Jesus foretells not only His departure but also His new coming. His exact words are: "I will not leave you desolate; I will come to you" (Jn 14:18). And at the moment of His final farewell before He ascends into heaven, He will repeat even more explicitly: "Lo, I am with you," and this [will be] "always, to the close of the age" (Mt 28:20).

This new coming of Christ, this continuous coming of His, in order to be with His Apostles, with the Church... occurs by the power of the Holy Spirit, who makes it possible for Christ, who has gone away, to come now and for ever in a new way. This new coming of Christ by the power of the Holy Spirit, and His constant presence and action in the spiritual life, are accomplished in the sacramental reality. In this reality, Christ, who has gone away in His visible humanity, comes, is present, and acts in the Church in such an intimate way as to make it His own Body. As such, the Church lives, works, and grows "to the close of the age." All this happens through the power of the Holy Spirit. [DV n. 61]

THE WEEK OF APRIL 26, 1998

17. THE CHURCH, GREAT SACRAMENT OF RECONCILIATION

According to our faith, the Word of God became flesh and came to dwell in the world.... By conquering through His death on the Cross evil and the power of sin, by His loving obedience, He brought salvation to all and became reconciliation for all. In Him God reconciled man to Himself....

The Church has the mission of proclaiming this reconciliation and as it were of being its sacrament in the world. The Church is the sacrament, that is to say, the sign and means of reconciliation, in different ways which differ in value but which all come together to obtain what the divine initiative of mercy desires to grant to humanity.

She is a sacrament in the first place by her very existence as a reconciled community which witnesses to and represents in the world the work of Christ.

She is also a sacrament through her service as the custodian and interpreter of sacred Scripture, which is the Good News of reconciliation inasmuch as it tells each succeeding generation about God's loving plan and shows to each generation the paths to universal reconciliation in Christ.

Finally, she is a sacrament by reason of the seven sacraments which, each in its own way, "make the Church."[3] For since they commemorate and renew Christ's Paschal Mystery, all the sacraments are a source of life for the Church, and in the Church's hands they are a means of conversion to God and of reconciliation among people. [RP n. 11]

18. THE CHURCH'S WORK OF RECONCILIATION

The mission of reconciliation is proper to the whole Church, also and especially to that Church which has already been admitted to the full sharing in divine glory with the Virgin Mary—the angels and the saints, who contemplate and adore the thrice-holy God. The Church in heaven, the Church on earth, and the Church in purgatory are mysteriously united in this cooperation with Christ in reconciling the world to God.

The first means of this [saving] action is that of prayer. It is certain that the Blessed Virgin, Mother of Christ and of the Church, and the saints, who have now reached the end of their earthly journey and possess God's glory, sustain by their intercession their brethren who are on pilgrimage through the world, in the commitment to conversion, to faith, to getting up again after every fall, to acting in order to help the growth of communion and peace in the Church and in the world. In the mystery of the communion of saints, universal reconciliation is accomplished in its most profound form, which is also the most fruitful for the salvation of all.

There is yet another means: that of preaching. The Church, since she is the disciple of the one Teacher Jesus Christ, in her own turn as mother and teacher untiringly exhorts people to reconciliation. And she does not hesitate to condemn the evil of sin, to proclaim the need for conversion, to invite and ask people to let themselves be reconciled. In fact, this is her prophetic mission in today's world, just as it was in the world of yesterday. It is the same mission as that of her Teacher and Head, Jesus. Like Him, the Church will always carry out this mission with sentiments of merciful love and will bring to all people those words of forgiveness and that invitation to hope which come from the Cross.

There is also the often so difficult and demanding means of pastoral action aimed at bringing back every individual—whoever and wherever he or she may be—to the path, at times a long one, leading back to the Father in the communion of all the brethren.

Finally, there is the means of witness, which is almost always silent. This is born from a twofold awareness on the part of the Church: that of being in herself "unfailingly holy,"[4] but also the awareness of the need to go forward and "daily be further purified and renewed, against the day when Christ will present her to Himself in all her glory without spot or wrinkle"—for, by reason of her sins, sometimes "the radiance of the Church's face shines less brightly" in the eyes of those who behold her.[5]

This witness cannot fail to assume two fundamental aspects. This first aspect is that of being the sign of that universal charity which Jesus Christ left as an inheritance to His followers, as a proof of belonging to His Kingdom. The second aspect is [her] translation into ever-new manifestations of conversion and reconciliation both within the Church and outside her, by the overcoming of tensions, by mutual forgiveness, by growth in the spirit of brotherhood and peace which is to be spread throughout the world. By this means the Church will effectively be able to work for the creation of what my predecessor Paul VI called the "civilization of love." [RP n. 12]

THE WEEK OF MAY 10, 1998

19. THE CHURCH'S WITNESS TO MORAL TRUTH

The Church's teaching, and particularly her firmness in defending the universal and permanent validity of the precepts prohibiting intrinsically evil acts, is not

51

infrequently seen as the sign of an intolerable intransigence, particularly with regard to the enormously complex and conflict-filled situations present in the moral life of individuals and of society today. This intransigence is said to be in contrast with the Church's motherhood. The Church, one hears, is lacking in understanding and compassion.

But the Church's motherhood can never in fact be separated from her teaching mission, which she must always carry out as the faithful Bride of Christ, who is the Truth in person. "As teacher, she never tires of proclaiming the moral norm.... The Church is in no way the author or the arbiter of this norm. In obedience to the truth which is Christ, whose image is reflected in the nature and dignity of the human person, the Church interprets the moral norm and proposes it to all people of good will, without concealing its demands of radicalness and perfection."[6]

In fact, genuine understanding and compassion must mean love for the person, for his true good, for his authentic freedom. And this does not result, certainly, from concealing or weakening moral truth, but rather from proposing it in its most profound meaning as an outpouring of God's eternal wisdom, which we have received in Christ, and as a service to man, to the growth of his freedom and to the attainment of his happiness. Still, a clear and forceful presentation of moral truth can never be separated from a profound and heartfelt respect, born of that patient and trusting love which man always needs along his moral journey, a journey frequently wearisome on account of difficulties, weakness, and painful situations. [VS n. 95]

THE WEEK OF MAY 17, 1998

20. THE MEANING OF THE KINGDOM OF GOD

Nowadays the Kingdom [of God] is much spoken of, but not always in a way consonant with the thinking of the Church. In fact, there are ideas about salvation and mission which... are focused [exclusively] on humankind's earthly needs. In this view, the Kingdom tends to become something completely human and secularized; what counts are programs and struggles for a liberation which is socio-economic, political, and even cultural, but within a horizon that is closed to the transcendent. Without denying that on this level too there are values to be promoted, such a notion nevertheless remains within the confines of a kingdom of humankind, deprived of its authentic and profound dimensions. Such a view easily translates into [simply] one more ideology of purely earthly progress. The Kingdom of God, however, "is not of this world,... is not from the world" (Jn 18:36).

There are also conceptions which deliberately emphasize the Kingdom and which describe themselves as "Kingdom-centered." They stress the image of a Church which is not concerned about herself, but which is totally concerned with bearing witness to and serving the Kingdom. It is a "Church for others" just as Christ is the "man for others." The Church's task is described as though it had to proceed in two directions: on the one hand promoting such "values of the Kingdom" as peace, justice, freedom, brotherhood, etc., while on the other hand fostering dialogue between peoples, cultures, and religions, so that through a mutual enrichment they might help the world to be renewed and to journey ever closer toward the Kingdom.

Together with positive aspects, these conceptions often reveal negative aspects as well. First, they are silent about Christ... since, according to them, Christ cannot be understood by those who lack Christian faith, whereas different peoples, cultures, and religions are capable of finding common ground in the one divine reality, by whatever it is called. For the same reason they put great stress on the mystery of Creation, which is reflected in the diversity of cultures and beliefs, but they keep silent about the mystery of Redemption. Furthermore, the Kingdom, as they understand it, ends up leaving very little room either for the Church or undervaluing the Church....

This is not the Kingdom of God as we know it from [God's] revelation. The Kingdom cannot be detached either from Christ or from the Church. [MR n. 17, 18]

21. THE KINGDOM OF GOD IS A PERSON

Christ not only proclaimed the Kingdom, but in Him the Kingdom itself became present and was fulfilled. This happened not only through His words and deeds: "Above all,... the kingdom is made manifest in the very person of Christ, Son of God and Son of Man, who came 'to serve and to give his life as a ransom for many'" (Mk 10:45).[7]

The Kingdom of God is not a concept, a doctrine, or a program subject to free interpretation, but it is before all else *a person* with the face and name of Jesus of Nazareth, the image of the invisible God. If the Kingdom is separated from Jesus, it is no longer the Kingdom of God which He revealed. The result is a distortion of the meaning of the Kingdom, which runs the risk of being transformed into a purely human or ideological goal, and a distortion of the identity of Christ, who no longer appears as the Lord to whom everything must one day be subjected (see 1 Corinthians 15:27).

Likewise, one may not separate the Kingdom from the Church. It is true that the Church is not an end unto herself, since she is ordered toward the Kingdom of God of which she is the seed, sign, and instrument. Yet, while remaining distinct from Christ and the Kingdom, the Church is indissolubly united to both.

Christ endowed the Church, His Body, with the fullness of the benefits and means of salvation. The Holy Spirit dwells in her, enlivens her with His gifts and charisms, sanctifies, guides, and constantly renews her. The result is a unique and special relationship which—while not excluding the action of Christ and the Spirit outside the Church's visible boundaries—confers upon her a specific and necessary role. Hence the Church's special connection with the Kingdom of God and of Christ, which she has "the mission of announcing and inaugurating among all peoples."[8]

It is within this overall perspective that the reality of the Kingdom is understood. Certainly, the Kingdom demands the promotion of human values, as well as those which can be properly called evangelical, since they are intimately bound up with the "Good News." But this sort of promotion, which is at the heart of the Church, must not be detached from or opposed to other fundamental tasks, such as proclaiming Christ and the Gospel, and establishing and building up communities which make present and active within humankind the living image of the Kingdom. [RM n. 18-19]

22. THE IMPORTANCE OF THE PARISH

The ecclesial community, while always having a universal dimension, finds its most immediate and visible expression in the parish. It is there that the Church is seen locally. In a certain sense it is the Church living in the midst of the homes of her sons and daughters.

It is necessary that in light of the faith all rediscover the true meaning of the parish, that is, the place where the very mystery of the Church is present and at work, even if at times it might be scattered over vast territories or almost not to be found in crowded and chaotic modern sections of cities. The parish is not principally a structure, a territory, or a building, but rather "the family of God, a fellowship afire with a unifying spirit,"[9] "a familial and welcoming home,"[10] the "community of the faithful."[11]

Plainly and simply, the parish is founded on a theological reality because it is a eucharistic community. This means that the parish is a community properly suited for celebrating the Eucharist, the living source for its upbuilding and the sacramental bond of its being in full communion with the whole Church. Such suitableness is rooted in the fact that the parish is a community of faith and an organic community, that is, constituted by the ordained ministers and other Christians, in which the pastor—who represents the diocesan bishop—is the hierarchical bond with the entire particular Church....

In the present circumstances the lay faithful have the ability to do very much and, therefore, ought to do very much toward the growth of an authentic ecclesial communion in their parishes in order to reawaken missionary zeal toward nonbelievers and believers themselves who have abandoned the faith or grown lax in the Christian life.

If indeed the parish is the Church placed in the neighborhoods of humanity, it lives and is at work through being deeply inserted in human society and intimately bound up with its aspirations and its dramatic events. Oftentimes the social context, especially in certain countries and environments, is violently shaken by elements of disintegration and dehumanization. The individual is lost and disoriented, but there always remains in the human heart the desire to experience and cultivate caring and personal relationships.

The response to such a desire can come from the parish, when, with the lay faithful's participation, it adheres to its fundamental vocation and mission, that is, to be a place in the world for the community of believers to gather together as a sign and instrument of the vocation of all to communion: in a word, to be a house of welcome to all and a place of service to all, or, as Pope John XXIII was fond of saying, to be the "village fountain" to which all would have recourse in their thirst. [CL n. 26-27]

23. THE CHURCH NEEDS ONGOING CONVERSION

Only in Christ can men and women find answers to the ultimate questions that trouble them. Only in Christ can they fully understand their dignity as persons created and loved by God. Jesus Christ is "the only Son from the Father... full of grace and truth" (see John 1:14).

By keeping the Incarnation of the eternal Word before her eyes, the Church understands more fully her twofold nature—human and divine. She is the mystical Body of the Word made flesh. As such she is inseparably united with her Lord and is holy in a way that can never fail.

The Church is also the visible means which God uses to reconcile sinful humanity to Himself. She is the people of God making its pilgrim way to the Father's house. In this sense she is constantly in need of conversion and renewal, and her members must ever be challenged "to purify and renew themselves so that the sign of Christ can shine more brightly on [her] face."[12] Only when the Church generates works of genuine holiness and humble service do the words of Isaiah come true: "All nations shall stream toward her" (see Isaiah 2:2). [TPS 39/2, 1994, 89]

THE SACRAMENTS

The Holy Spirit, "the Lord, the Giver of life," gives that divine life of Christ to the Church through the sacraments.

24. THE HOLY SPIRIT AND THE SACRAMENTS

In every celebration of the Eucharist [Christ's] coming, His [saving] presence, is sacramentally realized: in the Sacrifice and in Communion. It is accomplished by the power of the Holy Spirit, as part of His own mission. Through the Eucharist the Holy Spirit accomplishes that "strengthening of the inner man" spoken of in the Letter to the Ephesians (see Ephesians 3:16)....

Through the individual sacraments the Church fulfills her [saving] ministry to man. This sacramental ministry, every time it is accomplished, brings with it the mystery of the departure of Christ through the Cross and the Resurrection, by virtue of which the Holy Spirit comes. He comes and works: He gives life. For the sacraments signify grace and confer grace: they signify life and give life. The Church is the visible dispenser of the sacred signs, while the Holy Spirit acts in them as the invisible dispenser of the life which they signify. Together with the Spirit, Christ Jesus is present and acting. [DV n. 62-63]

25. THE EUCHARIST, CENTER AND SUMMIT OF SACRAMENTAL LIFE

In the mystery of the Redemption, that is to say in Jesus Christ's saving work, the Church not only shares in the Gospel of her Master through fidelity to the word and service of truth, but she also shares, through a submission filled with hope and love, in the power of His redeeming action expressed and enshrined by Him in a sacramental form, especially in the Eucharist. The Eucharist is the center and summit of the whole of sacramental life, through which each Christian receives the saving power of the Redemption, beginning with the mystery of Baptism, in which we are buried into the death of Christ, in order to become sharers in His Resurrection, as the Apostle [Paul] teaches (see Romans 6:3-5).

In the light of this teaching, we see still more clearly the reason why the entire sacramental life of the Church and of each Christian reaches its summit and fullness in the Eucharist. For by Christ's will there is in this sacrament a continual renewing of the mystery of the sacrifice of Himself that Christ offered to the Father on the altar of the Cross. [This is] a sacrifice that the Father accepted, giving, in return for this total self-giving by His Son, who became "obedient unto death" (Phil 2:8), His own paternal gift—that is to say, the grant of new immortal life in the Resurrection, since the Father is the first Source and the Giver of life from the beginning. That new life, which involves the bodily glorification of the crucified Christ, became an efficacious sign of the new gift granted to humanity, the gift that is the Holy Spirit, through whom the divine life that the Father has in Himself and gives to His Son (see John 5:26; 1 John 5:11) is communicated to all men who are united with Christ. [RH n. 20]

26. THE CHURCH LIVES BY THE EUCHARIST

The Church lives by the Eucharist, by the fullness of this sacrament, the stupendous content and meaning of which have often been expressed in the Church's Magisterium from the most distant times down to our own days. However, we can say with certainty that—although this teaching is sustained by the acuteness of theologians, by men of deep faith and prayer, and by ascetics and mystics, in complete fidelity to the eucharistic mystery—it still reaches no more than the threshold.... [I]t is incapable of grasping and translating into words what the Eucharist is in all its fullness, what is expressed by it, and what is actuated by it.

Indeed, the Eucharist is the ineffable sacrament! The essential commitment and, above all, the visible grace and source of supernatural strength for the Church as the people of God is to persevere and advance constantly in eucharistic life and eucharistic piety and to develop spiritually in the climate of the Eucharist.

With all the greater reason, then, it is not permissible for us, in thought, life, or action, to take away from this truly most holy sacrament its full magnitude and its essential meaning. It is at one and the same time a Sacrifice-sacrament, a Communion-sacrament, and a Presence-sacrament. And, although it is true that the Eucharist always was and must continue to be the most profound revelation of the human brotherhood of Christ's disciples and confessors, it cannot be treated merely as an occasion for manifesting this brotherhood. When celebrating the sacrament of the Body and Blood of the Lord, the full magnitude of the divine mystery must be respected—as must the full meaning of this sacramental sign in which Christ is really present and is received, the soul is filled with grace, and the pledge of future glory is given. [RH n. 20]

27. THE EUCHARIST AND THE KINGDOM

The Kingdom of God becomes present above all in the celebration of the sacrament of the Eucharist, which is the Lord's Sacrifice. In that celebration the fruits of the earth and the work of human hands—the bread and wine—are transformed mysteriously, but really and substantially, through the power of the Holy Spirit and the words of the minister, into the Body and Blood of the Lord Jesus Christ, the Son of God and Son of Mary, through whom the Kingdom of the Father has been made present in our midst.

The goods of this world and the work of our hands—the bread and wine—serve for the coming of the definitive Kingdom, since the Lord, through His Spirit, takes them up into Himself in order to offer Himself to the Father and to offer us with Himself in the renewal of His one Sacrifice, which anticipates God's Kingdom and proclaims its final coming.

Thus the Lord unites us with Himself through the Eucharist—Sacrament and Sacrifice—and He unites us with Himself and with one another by a bond stronger than any natural union.... Thus united, He sends us into the whole world to bear witness, through faith and works, to God's love, preparing the coming of His Kingdom and anticipating it, though in the obscurity of the present time. [SRS n. 48]

28. EUCHARISTIC WORSHIP LEADS TO CHARITY

Eucharistic worship constitutes the soul of all

Christian life. In fact, Christian life is expressed in the fulfilling of the greatest commandment, that is to say, in the love of God and neighbor, and this love finds its source in the Blessed Sacrament, which is commonly called the Sacrament of Love.

The Eucharist signifies this charity, and therefore recalls it, makes it present, and at the same time brings it about. Every time that we consciously share in it, there opens in our souls a real dimension of that unfathomable love that includes everything that God has done and continues to do for us human beings, as Christ says: "My Father goes on working, and so do I" (see John 5:17).

Together with this unfathomable and free gift, which is charity revealed in its fullest degree in the saving sacrifice of the Son of God—the sacrifice of which the Eucharist is the indelible sign—there also springs up within us a lively response of love. We not only know love; we ourselves begin to love. We enter, so to speak, upon the path of love and along this path make progress.

Thanks to the Eucharist, the love that springs up within us from the Eucharist develops in us, becomes deeper and grows stronger. Eucharistic worship is therefore precisely the expression of that love which is the authentic and deepest characteristic of the Christian vocation. This worship springs from the love and serves the love to which we are all called in Jesus Christ.

A living fruit of this worship is the perfecting of the image of God that we bear within us, an image that corresponds to the one that Christ has revealed in us. As we thus become adorers of the Father "in spirit and truth" (Jn 4:23), we mature in an ever-fuller union with Christ, we are ever more united to Him, and—if one may use the expression—we are ever more in harmony with Him. [DC n. 5]

29. THE EUCHARIST, SCHOOL OF LOVE

The authentic sense of the Eucharist becomes of itself the school of active love for neighbor. We know that this is the true and full order of love that the Lord has taught us: "By this love you have for one another, everyone will know that you are my disciples" (see John 13:35). The Eucharist educates us to this love in a deeper way; it shows us, in fact, what value each person, our brother or sister, has in God's eyes, if Christ offers Himself equally to each one, under the species of bread and wine. If our eucharistic worship is authentic, it must make us grow in awareness of the dignity of each person. The awareness of that dignity becomes the deepest motive of our relationship with our neighbor.

We must also become particularly sensitive to all human suffering and misery, to all injustice and wrong, and seek the way to redress them effectively. Let us learn to discover with respect the truth about the inner self that becomes the dwelling place of God in the Eucharist. Christ comes into the hearts of our brothers and sisters and visits their consciences.

How the image of each and every one changes when we become aware of this reality, when we make it the subject of our reflections! The sense of the eucharistic mystery leads us to a love for our neighbor, to a love for every human being. [DC n. 6]

UNITY IN THE CHURCH

Reflection on the Spirit of love, who has been poured out on every member of the Church, should lead us to ponder how we can allow His love to overcome divisions within the Church.

THE WEEK OF JULY 26, 1998

30. CATHOLIC UNITY

The reflection of the faithful in the second year of preparation ought to focus particularly on the value of unity within the Church, to which the various gifts and charisms bestowed upon her by the Spirit are directed.... The unity of the Body of Christ is founded on the activity of the Spirit, guaranteed by the apostolic ministry and sustained by mutual love (see 1 Corinthians 13:1-8). This catechetical enrichment of the faith cannot fail to bring the members of the p eople of God to a more mature awareness of their own responsibilities, as well as to a more lively sense of the importance of ecclesial obedience. [TMA n. 47]

THE WEEK OF AUGUST 2, 1998

31. A CREDIBLE SIGN OF RECONCILIATION

United to Christ as a visible communion of persons, the Church must take as her model the early Christian community in Jerusalem, which devoted itself "to the apostles' teaching and fellowship, to the breaking of bread and the prayers" (Acts 2:42). If the Church is to be a credible sign of reconciliation to the world, all those who believe, whoever they may be, must be "of one heart and one soul" (Acts 4:32).

By your fraternal communion the world will know that you are Christ's disciples!

The members of the Catholic Church should take to heart the plea of St. Paul: always be "eager to maintain the unity of the Spirit in the bond of peace" (Eph 4:3). With gentleness and patience, revere the Church as Christ's beloved Bride who is ever vigorous and youthful. So many problems arise when people think of the Church as "theirs," when in fact she belongs to Christ. Christ and the Church are inseparably united as "one flesh" (see Ephesians 5:31). Our love for Christ finds its vital expression in our love for the Church. Polarization and destructive criticism have no place among "those who are of the household of faith" (Gal 6:10). [TPS 39/2, 1994, 89]

32. THE MYSTERY OF COMMUNION

We turn to the words of Jesus: "I am the true vine and my Father is the vinedresser.... Abide in me and I in you" (Jn 15:1,4, RSV). These simple words reveal the mystery of communion that serves as the unifying bond between the Lord and His disciples, between Christ and the baptized—a living and life-giving communion through which Christians no longer belong to themselves but are the Lord's very own, as the branches are one with the vine.

The communion of Christians with Jesus has the communion of God as Trinity—namely, the unity of the Son to the Father in the gift of the Holy Spirit—as its model and source, and is itself the means to achieve this communion. United to the Son in the

Spirit's bond of love, Christians are united to the Father.

Jesus continues: "I am the vine, you are the branches" (Jn 15:5). From the communion that Christians experience in Christ there immediately flows the communion which they experience with one another: all are branches of a single vine, namely, Christ. In this communion is the wonderful reflection and participation in the mystery of the intimate life of love in God as Trinity—Father, Son, and Holy Spirit, as revealed by the Lord Jesus. For this communion Jesus prays: "That they may all be one; even as you, Father, are in me, and I in you, that they also may be in us, so that the world may believe that you have sent me" (see John 17:21)....

Church communion then is a gift, a great gift of the Holy Spirit to be gratefully accepted by the lay faithful, and at the same time to be lived with a deep sense of responsibility. This is concretely realized through their participation in the life and mission of the Church, to whose service the lay faithful put their varied and complementary ministries and charisms. [CL n. 18, 20]

THE WEEK OF AUGUST 16, 1998

33. WE CANNOT REMAIN IN ISOLATION

A member of the lay faithful "can never remain in isolation from the community, but must live in a continual interaction with others, with a lively sense of fellowship, rejoicing in an equal dignity and common commitment to bring to fruition the immense treasure that each has inherited. The Spirit of the Lord gives a vast variety of charisms, inviting people to assume different ministries and forms of service and reminding them, as He reminds all people in their relationship in the Church, that what distinguishes persons is not an increase in dignity, but a special and complementary capacity for service.... Thus, the charisms, the ministries, the different forms of service exercised by the lay faithful exist in communion and on behalf of communion. They are treasures that complement one another for the good of all and are under the wise guidance of their pastors...."[13]

So as to render thanks to God for the great gift of Church communion—which is the reflection in time of the eternal and ineffable communion of the love of God, Three in One—we once again consider Jesus' words: "I am the vine, you are the branches" (Jn 15:5). The awareness of the gift ought to be accompanied by a strong sense of responsibility for its use: it is, in fact, a gift that, like the talent of the Gospel parable, must be put to work in the life of ever-increasing communion.

To be responsible for the gift of communion means, first of all, to be committed to overcoming each temptation to division and opposition that works against the Christian life with its responsibility in the apostolate. The cry of St. Paul continues to resound as a reproach to those who are wounding the Body of Christ: "What I mean is that each one of you says, 'I belong to Paul,' or... 'I belong to Cephas,' or 'I belong to Christ.' Is Christ divided?" (1 Cor 1:12-13).

No, rather let these words of the Apostle sound a persuasive call: "I appeal to you, brethren, by the name of our Lord Jesus Christ, that all of you agree and that there be no dissensions among you, but that you be united in the same mind and the same judgment" (1 Cor 1:10). Thus the life of Church communion will become a sign for all the world and a compelling force that will lead persons to faith in Christ: "That they may all be one; even as you, Father, are in me and I in you, that they also may be in us, so that the world may believe that you have sent me" (see John 17:21). In such a way communion leads to *mission*, and mission itself to communion. [CL n. 20]

34. PATHS TO UNITY IN THE CHURCH

In order to overcome conflicts and to ensure that normal tensions do not prove harmful to the unity of the Church, we must all apply ourselves to the Word of God. We must relinquish our own subjective views and seek the truth where it is to be found, namely in the Divine Word itself and in the authentic interpretation of that Word provided by the Magisterium of the Church. In this light, listening to one another; respect; refraining from all hasty judgments; patience; the ability to avoid subordinating the faith which unites to the opinions, fashions, and ideological choices which divide—these are all qualities of a dialogue within the Church which must be persevering, open, and sincere.

Obviously dialogue would not have these qualities and would not become a factor of reconciliation if the magisterium were not heeded and accepted. Thus actively engaged in seeking her own internal communion, the Catholic Church can address an appeal for reconciliation to the other churches with which there does not exist full communion, as well as to the other religions and even to all those who are seeking God with a sincere heart. [RP n. 25]

THE WEEK OF AUGUST 30, 1998

35. UNITY IS THE FRUIT OF CONVERSION
Unity is not the result of human policies or hidden and mysterious intentions. Instead, unity springs from conversion of the heart, and from sincere acceptance of the unchanging principles laid down by Christ for His Church. Particularly important among these principles is the effective communion of all the parts of the Church with her visible foundation: Peter, the Rock.

Consequently, a Catholic who wishes to remain such and to be recognized as such cannot reject the principle of communion with the successor of Peter. [TPS 40/3, 1995, 160]

CLERGY, RELIGIOUS, AND LAITY
The Holy Spirit has given different but complementary charisms and ministries to those in each state of the Christian life; all of them are necessary for the Church to fulfill her mission.

THE WEEK OF SEPTEMBER 6, 1998

36. A DIVERSITY OF GIFTS
All the members of the people of God—clergy, men and women religious, the lay faithful—are laborers in the vineyard... Every one of us possessing charisms

and ministries, diverse yet complementary, works in the one and the same vineyard of the Lord. Simply in *being* Christians, even before actually *doing* the works of a Christian, all are branches of the one fruitful vine which is Christ. All are living members of the one Body of the Lord built up through the power of the Spirit....

The states of life, by being ordered one to the other, are thus bound together among themselves. They all share in a deeply basic meaning: that of being the manner of living out the commonly shared Christian dignity and the universal call to holiness in the perfection of love. They are different yet complementary in the sense that each of them has a basic and unmistakable character which sets each apart, while at the same time each of them is seen in relation to the other and placed at each other's service.

Thus the *lay* state of life has its distinctive feature in its secular character. It fulfills an ecclesial service in bearing witness and, in its own way, recalling for priests [and] women and men religious the significance of the earthly and temporal realities in the [saving] plan of God. In turn, the *ministerial* priesthood represents, in different times and places, the permanent guarantee of the sacramental presence of Christ the Redeemer. The *religious* state bears witness to the . . . straining toward the Kingdom of God that is prefigured and in some way anticipated and experienced even now through the vows of chastity, poverty, and obedience.

All the states of life, whether taken collectively or individually in relation to the others, are at the service of the Church's growth. While different in expression they are deeply united in the Church's mystery of communion and are dynamically coordinated in its unique mission. Thus in the diversity of the states of life and the variety of vocations this same unique mystery of the Church reveals and experiences anew the infinite richness of the mystery of Jesus Christ. [CL n. 55]

37. PRAY AND WORK FOR VOCATIONS

"I will give you shepherds after my own heart" (Jer 3:15). Today, this promise of God is still living and at work in the Church. At all times, she knows she is the fortunate receiver of these prophetic words. She sees them put into practice daily in so many parts of the world, or rather, in so many human hearts, young hearts in particular. On the threshold of the third millennium, and in the face of the serious and urgent needs which confront the Church and the world, she yearns to see this promise fulfilled in a new and richer way, more intensely and effectively. She hopes for an extraordinary outpouring of the Spirit of Pentecost.

The Lord's promise calls forth from the heart of the Church a prayer that is a confident and burning petition in the love of the Father, who—just as He has sent Jesus the Good Shepherd, the Apostles, their successors, and a countless host of priests—will continue to show to the people of today his faithfulness, his goodness.

And the Church is ready to respond to this grace. She feels in her heart that God's gift begs for a united and generous reply. The entire people of God should pray and work tirelessly for priestly vocations. Candidates for the priesthood should prepare themselves very conscientiously to welcome God's gift and put it into practice, knowing that the Church and the world have an absolute need of them. They should deepen their love for Christ the Good Shepherd, pattern their hearts on His, be ready to go out as His image into the highways of the world to proclaim to all mankind Christ the Way, the Truth, and the Life.

I appeal especially to families. May parents, mothers in particular, be generous in giving their sons to the Lord when He calls them to the priesthood. May they cooperate joyfully in their vocational journey, realizing that in this way they will be increasing and deepening their Christian fruitfulness in the Church and that, in a sense, they will experience the blessedness of Mary, the Virgin Mother: "Blessed are you among women, and blessed is the fruit of your womb!" (Lk 1:42).

To today's young people I say: Be docile to the voice of the Spirit, let the great expectations of the Church, of mankind, resound in the depths of your hearts. Do not be afraid to open your minds to Christ the Lord who is calling. Feel His loving look upon you and respond enthusiastically to Jesus when He asks you to follow Him without reserve. [PDV n. 82]

THE WEEK OF SEPTEMBER 20, 1998

38. THE CLERGY:
A GRACE FOR THE WHOLE CHURCH

The ministries which exist and are at work at this time in the Church are all—even in their variety of forms—a participation in Jesus Christ's own ministry as the Good Shepherd who lays down His life for the sheep (see John 10:11), the humble servant who gives Himself without reserve for the salvation of all (see Mark 10:45). The Apostle Paul is quite clear in speaking about the ministerial constitution of the Church in apostolic times. In his First Letter to the Corinthians he writes: "And God has appointed in the Church first apostles, second prophets, third teachers..." (1 Cor 12:28)....

In a primary position in the Church are the ordained ministries, that is, the ministries that come from the Sacrament of Orders. In fact, with the mandate to make disciples of all nations (see Matthew 28:19), the Lord Jesus chose and constituted the Apostles—seed of the People of the New Covenant and origin of the hierarchy—to form and to rule the priestly people. The mission of the Apostles, which the Lord Jesus continues to entrust to the pastors of His people, is a true service, significantly referred to in Sacred Scripture as... service or ministry.

The ministries receive the charism of the Holy Spirit from the risen Christ in uninterrupted succession from the Apostles, through the Sacrament of Orders. From Him they receive the authority and sacred power to serve the Church, acting... in the person of Christ, the Head, and to gather her in the Holy Spirit through the Gospel and the sacraments.

The ordained ministries, apart from the persons who receive them, are a grace for the entire Church. These ministries express and realize a participation in the priesthood of Jesus Christ that is different, not simply in degree but in essence, from the participation given to all the lay faithful through Baptism and Confirmation. On the other hand, the ministerial priesthood... essentially has the royal priesthood of all the faithful as its aim and is ordered to it.

For this reason, so as to assure and to increase communion in the Church, particularly in those places where there is a diversity and complementarity of ministries, pastors must always acknowledge that their ministry is fundamentally ordered to the service of the entire people of God (see Hebrews 5:1). The lay faithful, in turn, must acknowledge that the ministerial priesthood is totally necessary for their participation in the mission of the Church.

The Church's mission of salvation in the world is realized not only by the ministers in virtue of the Sacrament of Orders but also by all the lay faithful.... The pastors, therefore, ought to acknowledge and foster the ministries, the offices, and roles of the lay faithful that find their foundation in the Sacraments of Baptism and Confirmation, indeed, for a good many of them, in the Sacrament of Matrimony. [CL n. 21-22]

THE WEEK OF SEPTEMBER 27, 1998

39. PRIESTS REPRESENT CHRIST

Priests are called to prolong the presence of Christ, the one high priest, embodying His way of life and making Him visible in the midst of the flock entrusted to their care. We find this clearly and precisely stated in the First Letter of Peter: "I exhort the elders among you as a fellow elder and a witness of the sufferings of Christ as well as a partaker in the glory that is to be revealed. Tend the flock of God that is your charge, not by constraint but willingly, not for shameful gain but eagerly, not as domineering over those in your charge but being examples to the flock. And when the Chief Shepherd is manifested you will obtain the unfading crown of glory" (1 Pt 5:1-4).

In the Church and on behalf of the Church, priests are a sacramental representation of Jesus Christ—the Head and Shepherd—authoritatively proclaiming His word, repeating His acts of forgiveness and His offer of salvation, particularly in Baptism, Penance, and the Eucharist, showing His loving concern to the point of a total gift of self for the flock, which they gather into unity and lead to the Father through Christ and in the Spirit. In a word, priests exist and act in order to proclaim the Gospel to the world and to build up the Church in the name and person of Christ the Head and Shepherd.

This is the ordinary and proper way in which ordained ministers share in the one priesthood of Christ. By the sacramental anointing of Holy Orders, the Holy Spirit configures them in a new and special way to Jesus Christ the Head and Shepherd. He forms and strengthens them with His pastoral charity. And He gives them an authoritative role in the Church as servants of the proclamation of the Gospel to every people and of the fullness of Christian life of all the baptized. [PDV n. 15-16]

THE WEEK OF OCTOBER 4, 1998

40. ON THE SHORTAGE OF PRIESTS

Our times consume and require ever-greater priestly energy. However, although many parts of the world are experiencing a great blossoming of vocations, in other areas one notices a persistent shortage of priests and the phenomenon of a great many sacred ministers of advanced age, ill, or worn out by the evermore whirling pace of apostolic ministry. As a result, even where the number of ordinations and seminarians has increased, the availability of priests is still insufficient to meet all needs.

Hence the demand is felt for an appropriate collaboration of the lay faithful in the pastoral ministry of priests, while always respecting, logically, the sacramental limits and the difference of charisms and ecclesial roles.... [But] the particular gift of each of the Church's members must be wisely and carefully acknowledged, safeguarded, promoted, discerned, and coordinated, without confusing roles, functions, or theological or canonical status. Otherwise the Body of Christ is not built up nor does its mission of salvation correctly develop.... We cannot increase the communion and unity of the Church by clericalizing the lay faithful or by laicizing priests.

As a consequence, we cannot offer the lay faithful experiences and ways of participating in the pastoral ministry of priests that would in any way or to any degree entail a theoretical or practical misconception of the unchangeable differences willed by Christ and the Holy Spirit for the good of the Church: the diversity of vocations and states of life, the diversity of ministries, charisms, and responsibilities.... It should also be understood that these clarifications and distinctions do not stem from a concern to defend clerical privileges, but from the need to be obedient to the will of Christ and to respect the constitutive form which He indelibly impressed on His Church....

Above all, it must never be forgotten that problems caused by the shortage of ordained ministers can be alleviated only secondarily or temporarily by having lay people in some way supply for them. The shortage of sacred ministers can be avoided only by "praying the Lord of the harvest to send out laborers into his harvest" (see Matthew 9:38), giving the primacy to God and caring for the identity and holiness of the priests there are. This is simply the logic of faith! Every Christian community that lives its total dedication to Christ and remains open to His grace will obtain from Him precisely those vocations which serve to represent Him as the Shepherd of His people.

Where there is a shortage of these vocations, the essential problem is not to search for alternatives— and God forbid that they should be sought by distorting His wise plan—but to focus all the efforts of the Christian people on making the voice of Christ, who never stops calling, heard again in families, parishes, Catholic schools, and communities. [TPS 39/5, 1994, 309-12]

THE WEEK OF OCTOBER 11, 1998

41. PRIESTS WILL CONTINUE TO THE END OF TIME

There is an essential aspect of the priest that does not change: the priest of tomorrow, no less than the priest of today, must resemble Christ. When Jesus lived on this earth, He manifested in Himself the definitive role of the priest by establishing a ministerial priesthood with which the Apostles were the first to be invested. This priesthood is destined to last in endless succession throughout history.

In this sense, the priest of the third millennium will continue the work of the priests who, in the preceding millennia, have animated the life of the Church. In the third millennium the priestly vocation will continue to be the call to live the unique and permanent priesthood of Christ. [PDV n. 5]

42. THE LAY FAITHFUL: CALLED TO HOLINESS

We come to a full sense of the dignity of the lay faithful if we consider the prime and fundamental vocation that the Father assigns to each of them in Jesus Christ through the Holy Spirit: the vocation to holiness, that is, the perfection of charity. Holiness is the greatest testimony of the dignity conferred on a disciple of Christ....

The Church... is the choice vine whose branches live and grow with the same holy and life-giving energies that come from Christ. She is the Mystical Body whose members share in the same life of holiness of the Head who is Christ. She is the beloved spouse of the Lord Jesus who delivered Himself up for her sanctification (see Ephesians 5:25ff). The Spirit that sanctified the human nature of Jesus in Mary's virginal womb (see Luke 1:35) is the same Spirit that is abiding and working in the Church to communicate to her the holiness of the Son of God made man.

It is evermore urgent that today all Christians take up again the way of the Gospel renewal, welcoming in a spirit of generosity the invitation expressed by the Apostle Peter "to be holy in all conduct" (see 1

Peter 1:15).... Everyone in the Church, precisely because they are members, receives and thereby shares in the common vocation to holiness. In the fullness of this title and on equal par with all other members of the Church, the lay faithful are called to holiness....

The call to holiness is rooted in Baptism and proposed anew in the other sacraments, principally in the Eucharist. Since Christians are reclothed in Christ Jesus and refreshed by His Spirit, they are "holy." They therefore have the ability to manifest this holiness and the responsibility to bear witness to it in all that they do. The Apostle Paul never tires of admonishing all Christians to live "as is fitting among saints" (Eph 5:3).

Life according to the Spirit, whose fruit is holiness (see Romans 6:22; Galatians 5:22), stirs up every baptized person and requires each to follow and imitate Jesus Christ in embracing the Beatitudes; in listening and meditating on the Word of God; in conscious and active participation in the liturgical and sacramental life of the Church; in personal prayer; in family or in community; in the hunger and thirst for justice; in the practice of the commandment of love in all circumstances of life and service to the brethren, especially the least, the poor, and the suffering. [CL n. 16]

THE WEEK OF OCTOBER 25, 1998

43. THE CHARISMS OF THE HOLY SPIRIT

The Holy Spirit, while bestowing diverse ministries in Church communion, enriches it still further with particular gifts or promptings of grace, called *charisms*. These can take a great variety of forms both as a manifestation of the absolute freedom of the Spirit who abundantly supplies them and as a response to the varied needs of the Church in history. The description and the classification given to these gifts in the New Testament are an indication of their rich variety.

"To each [writes the Apostle Paul] is given the manifestation of the Spirit for the common good. To one is given through the Spirit the utterance of wisdom, and to another the utterance of knowledge according to the same Spirit, to another faith by the same Spirit, to another gifts of healing by the one Spirit, to another the working of miracles, to another prophecy, to another the ability to distinguish between spirits, to another various kinds of tongues, to another the interpretation of tongues" (1 Cor 12:7-10; see also 12:4-6, 28-31; Romans 12:6-8; 1 Peter 4:10-11).

Whether they be exceptional and great or simple and ordinary, the charisms are graces of the Holy Spirit that have, directly or indirectly, a usefulness for the ecclesial community, ordered as they are to the building up of the Church, to the well-being of humanity, and to the needs of the world.

Even in our own times there is no lack of a fruitful manifestation of various charisms among the faithful, women and men. These charisms are given to individual persons and can be shared by others in such ways as to continue in time a precious and effective heritage, serving as a source of a particular spiritual affinity among persons....

The gifts of the Spirit demand that those who have received them exercise them for the growth of the whole Church. The charisms are received in gratitude both on the part of the one who receives them and also on the part of the entire Church. They are in fact a singularly rich source of grace for the vitality of the apostolate and for the holiness of the whole Body of Christ, provided that they be gifts that come truly from the Spirit and are exercised in full conformity with the authentic promptings of the Spirit. In this sense the discernment of charisms is always necessary....No charism dispenses a person from reference and submission to the pastors of the Church. [CL n. 24]

THE WEEK OF NOVEMBER 1, 1998

44. LAY PARTICIPATION AND COOPERATION IN CHURCH AFFAIRS

Lay people, "by reason of the knowledge, competence, or outstanding ability which they enjoy, are able and sometimes even obliged to express their opinion on things which concern the good of the Church."[14] They can do this either individually or through appropriate bodies. It is therefore incumbent upon the Church's pastors to be attentive to the suggestions and proposals of the lay faithful, while at the same time exercising the freedom and authority which is theirs by divine right to shepherd that part of God's people entrusted to them.

It would be an error to judge ecclesial structures of participation and cooperation by secular democratic standards, or to consider them as forms of "power-sharing" or means of imposing partisan ideas or interests. They should be looked on as forms of spiritual solidarity proper to the Church as a communion of persons who, "though many, are one body in Christ, and individually members one of another" (Rom 12:5). Such structures are fruitful to the extent that they manifest the true nature of the Church as a hierarchical communion, animated and guided by the Holy Spirit. [TPS 39/2, 1994, 122]

EVANGELIZATION AND MISSION

Christ promised to pour out the Holy Spirit upon His followers so that they would "receive power" for the mission He had given them: to be His "witnesses... to the end of the earth" (Acts 1:8).

THE WEEK OF NOVEMBER 8, 1998

45. THE URGENCY OF MISSIONARY ACTIVITY

The mission of Christ the Redeemer, which is entrusted to the Church, is still very far from completion. As the second millennium after Christ's coming draws to an end, an overall view of the human race shows that this mission is still only beginning and that we must commit ourselves wholeheartedly to its service. It is the Spirit who impels us to proclaim the great works of God: "For if I preach the Gospel, that gives me no ground for boasting. For necessity is laid upon me. Woe to me if I do not preach the Gospel!" (1 Cor 9:16)....

There is a new awareness that missionary activity is a matter for all Christians, for all dioceses and parishes, Church institutions and associations. Nevertheless, in

this new springtime of Christianity there is an undeniable negative tendency.... Missionary activity
specifically directed "to the nations" (*ad gentes*)
appears to be waning, and this tendency is certainly
not in line with the directives of the [Second
Vatican] Council and of subsequent statements of
the Magisterium. Difficulties both internal and exter-
nal have weakened the Church's missionary thrust
toward non-Christians, a fact which must arouse concern among all who believe in Christ. For in the
Church's history, missionary drive has always been a
sign of vitality, just as its lessening is a sign of a crisis
of faith....

I wish to invite the Church to renew her missionary commitment.... For missionary activity renews
the Church, revitalizes faith and Christian identity,
and offers fresh enthusiasm and new incentive. Faith
is strengthened when it is given to others! It is in
commitment to the Church's universal mission that
the new evangelization of Christian peoples will find
inspiration and support.

But what moves me even more strongly to proclaim the urgency of missionary evangelization is the
fact that it is the primary service which the Church
can render to every individual and to all humanity in
the modern world, a world which has experienced
marvelous achievements but which seems to have lost
its sense of ultimate realities and of existence itself....

Peoples everywhere, open the doors to Christ! His
Gospel in no way detracts from the human person's
freedom, from the respect that is owed to every culture, and to whatever is good in each religion. By
accepting Christ, you open yourselves to the definitive

Word of God, to the One in whom God has made Himself fully known and has shown us the path to Himself. [RM n. 1-3]

46. NEW OPPORTUNITIES FOR EVANGELIZATION

The number of those who do not know Christ and do not belong to the Church is constantly on the increase. Indeed, since the end of the [Second Vatican] Council it has almost doubled. When we consider this immense portion of humanity which is loved by the Father and for whom He sent His Son, the urgency of the Church's mission is obvious.

On the other hand, our own times offer the Church new opportunities in this field. We have witnessed the collapse of oppressive ideologies and political systems; the opening of frontiers and the formation of a more united world due to an increase in communications; the affirmation among peoples of the Gospel values which Jesus made incarnate in His own life (peace, justice, brotherhood, concern for the needy); and a kind of soulless economic and technical development which only stimulates the search for the truth about God, about man, and about the meaning of life itself.

God is opening before the Church the horizons of a humanity more fully prepared for the sowing of the Gospel. I sense that the moment has come to commit all of the Church's energies to a new evangelization and to the mission *ad gentes*. No believer in Christ, no institution of the Church, can avoid this supreme duty: to proclaim Christ to all peoples. [RM 3]

47. LAY HOLINESS AND LAY MISSION

The vocation of the lay faithful to holiness implies that life according to the Spirit expresses itself in a particular way in their involvement in temporal affairs and in their participation in earthly activities. Once again the Apostle admonishes us: "Whatever you do, in word or deed, do everything in the name of the Lord Jesus, giving thanks to God the Father through him" (Col 3:17)....

The vocation to holiness must be recognized and lived by the lay faithful, first of all as an undeniable and demanding obligation and as a shining example of the infinite love of the Father that has regenerated them in His own life of holiness. Such a vocation, then, ought to be called an essential and inseparable element of the new life of Baptism, and therefore an element which determines their dignity. At the same time the vocation to holiness is intimately connected to mission and to the responsibility entrusted to the lay faithful in the Church and in the world. In fact, that same holiness, which is derived simply from their participation in the Church's holiness, represents their first and fundamental contribution to the building of the Church herself, who is the "Communion of Saints."

The eyes of faith behold a wonderful scene: that of a countless number of lay people, both women and men, busy at work in their daily life and activity, oftentimes far from view and quite unacclaimed by the world, unknown to the world's great personages but nonetheless looked upon in love by the Father, untiring laborers who work in the Lord's vineyard.

Confident and steadfast through the power of God's grace, these are the humble yet great builders of the Kingdom of God in history. [CL n. 17]

48. SHARERS IN CHRIST'S MISSION

The lay faithful are sharers in the *priestly mission* for which Jesus offered Himself on the Cross and continues to be offered in the celebration of the Eucharist for the glory of God and the salvation of humanity. Incorporated in Jesus Christ, the baptized are united to Him and to His sacrifice in the offering they make of themselves and their daily activities (see Romans 12:1-2)....

Through their participation in the *prophetic mission* of Christ, "who proclaimed the kingdom of his Father by the testimony of his life and by the power of his word,"[15] the lay faithful are given the ability and responsibility to accept the Gospel in faith and to proclaim it in word and deed, without hesitating to courageously identify and denounce evil. United to Christ, the "great prophet" (Luke 7:16), and in the Spirit made witnesses of the risen Christ, the lay faithful are made sharers in the appreciation of the Church's supernatural faith, that "cannot err in matters of belief,"[16] and sharers as well in the grace of the Word (see Acts 2:17-18; Revelation 19:10). They are also called to allow the newness and the power of the Gospel to shine out every day in their family and social life, as well as to express patiently and courageously in the contradictions of the present age their hope of future glory even "through the framework of their secular life."[17]

87

Because the lay faithful belong to Christ, Lord and King of the Universe, they share in His *kingly mission* and are called by Him to spread that Kingdom in history. They exercise their kingship as Christians, above all in the spiritual combat in which they seek to overcome in themselves the kingdom of sin (see Romans 6:12)—and then to make a gift of themselves so as to serve, in justice and in charity, Jesus who is Himself present in all His brothers and sisters, above all in the very least (see Matthew 25:40).

But in particular the lay faithful are called to restore to creation all its original value. In ordering creation to the authentic well-being of humanity in an activity governed by the life of grace, they share in the exercise of the power with which the risen Christ draws all things to Himself and subjects them along with Himself to the Father, so that God might be everything to everyone (see 1 Corinthians 15:28; John 12:32). [CL n. 14-15]

THE WEEK OF DECEMBER 6, 1998

49. Evangelization Is the Task of Every Christian

By her very nature the Church is a missionary community. She is continually impelled by this missionary thrust which she has received from the Holy Spirit on the day of Pentecost: "You will receive power when the Holy Spirit comes upon you, and you will be my witnesses" (Acts 1:8, NAB). In fact, the Holy Spirit is the principal agent of the Church's entire mission.

As a consequence, the Christian vocation is also directed toward the apostolate, toward evangelization, toward mission. All baptized persons are called by Christ to become His apostles in their own personal situation and in the world: "As the Father has sent me, so I send you" (Jn 20:21, NAB). Through His Church Christ entrusts you with the fundamental mission of sharing with others the gift of salvation, and He invites you to participate in building His Kingdom. He chooses you, in spite of the personal limitations everyone has, because He loves you and believes in you. This unconditional love of Christ should be the very soul of your apostolic work, in accord with the words of St. Paul: "The love of Christ impels us" (2 Cor 5:14, NAB).

Being disciples of Christ is not a private matter. On the contrary, the gift of faith must be shared with others. For this reason the same Apostle writes, "If I preach the gospel, this is no reason for me to boast, for an obligation has been imposed on me, and woe to me if I do not preach it!" (1 Cor 9:16, NAB). Moreover, do not forget that faith is strengthened and grows precisely when it is given to others.

The mission lands in which you have been called to work are not necessarily located in distant countries, but can be found throughout the world, even in the everyday situations where you are. In the countries of more ancient Christian tradition today there is an urgent need to call attention again to the message of Jesus by means of a new evangelization, since there are widespread groups of people who do not know Christ, or do not know Him well enough. Many, caught by the mechanisms of secularism and religious indifference, are far from Him. [TPS 37/3, 1992, 139-40]

50. PROCLAIMING CHRIST

Proclaiming Christ means above all giving witness to Him with one's life. It is the simplest form of preaching the Gospel and, at the same time, the most effective way available to you. It consists of showing the visible presence of Christ in one's own life by a daily commitment and by making every concrete decision in conformity with the Gospel. Today the world especially needs believable witnesses....

Therefore, testify to your faith through your involvement in the world, too. A disciple of Christ is never a passive and indifferent observer of what is taking place. On the contrary, he feels responsible for transforming social, political, economic, and cultural reality.

Moreover, proclaiming means precisely proclaiming—becoming one who brings the word of salvation to others. There is indeed much ignorance about the Christian faith, but there is also a deep desire to hear the Word of God. And faith comes from listening.

St. Paul writes: "And how can they believe unless they have heard of him?" (see Romans 10:14).... Proclaiming the Word of God is not the responsibility of priests or religious alone, but it is yours, too. You must have the courage to speak about Christ in your families and in places where you study, work, or recreate, inspired with the same fervor the Apostles had when they said, "We cannot help speaking of what we have heard and seen" (see Acts 4:20). Nor should you be silent! There are places and circumstances where you alone can bring the seed of God's word.

Do not be afraid of presenting Christ to someone who does not yet know Him. Christ is the true answer, the most complete answer to all the questions which concern the human person and his destiny. Without Christ, the human person remains an unsolvable riddle. Therefore, have the courage to present Christ! Certainly, you must do this in a way which respects each person's freedom of conscience, but you must do it. Helping a brother or sister to discover Christ, the Way, the Truth, and the Life (see John 14:6), is a true act of love for one's neighbor. [TPS 37/3, 1992, 140-1]

THE WEEK OF DECEMBER 20, 1998

51. WITNESS, THE FIRST FORM OF EVANGELIZATION

People today put more trust in witnesses than in teachers, in experience than in teaching, and in life and action than in theories. The witness of a Christian life is the first and irreplaceable form of mission: Christ, whose mission we continue, is the "witness" *par excellence* (see Revelation 1:5; 3:14) and the model of all Christian witness. The Holy Spirit accompanies the Church along her way and associates her with the witness He gives to Christ (see John 15:26-27).

The first form of witness is the very life of the missionary, of the Christian family, and of the ecclesial community, which reveal a new way of living. The missionary who, despite all his or her human limitations and defects, lives a simple life, taking Christ as the model, is a sign of God and of transcendent realities. But everyone in the Church, striving to imitate the Divine Master, can and must bear this kind of witness; in many cases it is the only possible way of being a missionary.

The evangelical witness which the world finds most appealing is that of concern for people and of charity toward the poor, the weak, and those who suffer. The complete generosity underlying this attitude and these actions stands in marked contrast to human selfishness. It raises precise questions which lead to God and to the Gospel. A commitment to peace, to justice, human rights, and human promotion is also a witness to the Gospel when it is a sign of concern for persons and is directed toward integral human development.

Christians and Christian communities are very much a part of the life of their respective nations and can be a sign of the Gospel in their fidelity to their native land, people, and national culture, while always preserving the freedom brought by Christ.... [But] the Church is [also] called to bear witness to Christ by taking courageous and prophetic stands in the face of the corruption of political or economic power; by not seeking her own glory and material wealth; by using her resources to serve the poorest of the poor and by imitating Christ's own simplicity of life. The Church and her missionaries must also bear the witness of humility, above all with regard to themselves—a humility which allows them to make a personal and communal examination of conscience in order to correct in their behavior whatever is contrary to the Gospel and disfigures the face of Christ. [RM n. 42-43]

52. A NEW MISSIONARY ADVENT

The number of those awaiting Christ is still immense: the human and cultural groups not yet reached by the Gospel, or for whom the Church is scarcely present, are so widespread as to require the uniting of all the Church's resources. As she prepares to celebrate the Jubilee of the year 2000, the whole Church is even more committed to a new missionary advent. We must increase our apostolic zeal to pass on to others the light and joy of the faith, and to this high ideal the whole people of God must be educated.

We cannot be content when we consider the millions of our brothers and sisters, who like us have been redeemed by the blood of Christ, but who live in ignorance of the love of God. For each believer, as for the entire Church, the missionary task must remain foremost, for it concerns the eternal destiny of humanity and corresponds to God's mysterious and merciful plan. [RM n. 86]

A FINAL WORD ON THE GREAT JUBILEE

I invite the faithful to raise to the Lord fervent prayers to obtain the light and assistance necessary for the preparation and celebration of the forthcoming Jubilee. I exhort my Venerable Brothers in the Episcopate and the ecclesial communities entrusted to them to open their hearts to the promptings of the Spirit. He will not fail to arouse enthusiasm and lead people to celebrate the Jubilee with renewed faith and generous participation.

I entrust this responsibility of the whole Church to the maternal intercession of Mary, Mother of the Redeemer. She, the Mother of Fairest Love, will be for Christians on the way to the Great Jubilee of the third millennium the star which safely guides their steps to the Lord. May the unassuming young woman of Nazareth, who two thousand years ago offered to the world the Incarnate Word, lead the men and women of the new millennium toward the One who is "the true light that enlightens every man" (Jn 1:9). [TMA n. 59]

AS THE THIRD MILLENNIUM DRAWS NEAR

(The complete official text of the apostolic letter
Tertio Millennio Adveniente by His Holiness
Pope John Paul II, released on November 14, 1994.)

To the Bishops, Priests and Deacons, Men and
Women Religious, and All the Lay Faithful

INTRODUCTION

1. As the third millennium of the new era draws near, our thoughts turn spontaneously to the words of the Apostle Paul, "When the fullness of time had come, God sent forth his Son, born of woman" (Gal 4:4). *The fullness of time coincides with the mystery of the Incarnation of the Word,* of the Son who is of one being with the Father, and with the mystery of the Redemption of the world. In this passage, St. Paul emphasizes that the Son of God was born of woman, born under the Law, and came into the world in order to redeem all who were under the Law so that they might receive adoption as sons and daughters. And he adds, "Because you are sons, God has sent the Spirit of his Son into our hearts, crying 'Abba! Father!'" His conclusion is truly comforting: "So through God you are no longer a slave but a son, and if a son then an heir" (Gal 4:6-7).

Paul's presentation of the mystery of the Incarnation contains *the Revelation of the mystery of the Trinity and the continuation of the Son's mission in the mission of the Holy Spirit.* The Incarnation of the Son of God, His conception and birth, is the prerequisite for the sending of the Holy Spirit. This text of St. Paul *thus allows the fullness of the mystery of the Redemptive Incarnation to shine forth.*

I
"JESUS CHRIST IS THE SAME YESTERDAY AND TODAY"
(Heb 13:8)

2. In his Gospel Luke has handed down to us a *concise narrative of the circumstances of Jesus' birth:* "In those days a decree went out from Caesar Augustus that all the world should be enrolled.... And all went to be enrolled, each to his own city. And Joseph also went up from Galilee, from the city of Nazareth, to Judea, to the city of David, which is called Bethlehem, because he was of the house and lineage of David, to be enrolled with Mary, his betrothed, who was with child. And while they were there, the time came for her to be delivered. And she gave birth to her first-born son and wrapped him in swaddling cloths, and laid him in a manger, because there was no place for them in the inn" (Lk 2:1, 3-7).

Thus was fulfilled what the Angel Gabriel foretold at the Annunciation, when he spoke to the Virgin of Nazareth in these words: "Hail, full of grace, the Lord is with you" (Lk 1:28). Mary was troubled by these words, and so the divine messenger quickly added: "Do not be afraid, Mary, for you have found favor with God. And behold, you will conceive in your womb and bear a son, and you shall call his name Jesus. He will be great and will be called the Son of the Most High.... The Holy Spirit will come upon you and the power of the Most High will overshadow you; therefore the child to be born will be called holy, the Son of God" (Lk 1:30-32, 35). Mary's reply to the angel was unhesitating: "Behold, I am

100

the handmaid of the Lord; let it be to me according to your word" (Lk 1:38). Never in human history did so much depend, as it did then, upon the consent of one human creature.[1]

3. John, in the Prologue of his Gospel, captures in one phrase all the depth of the mystery of the Incarnation. He writes, *"And the Word became flesh and dwelt among us,* full of grace and truth; we have beheld his glory, glory as of the only Son from the Father" (1:14, RSV). For John, the Incarnation of the Eternal Word, of one being with the Father, took place in the conception and birth of Jesus. The Evangelist speaks of the Word who in the beginning was with God, and through whom everything which exists was made; the Word in whom was life, the life which was the light of men (cf. 1:1-4). Of the only-begotten Son, God from God, the Apostle Paul writes that He is *"the first-born of all creation"* (Col 1:15). God created the world through the Word. The Word is Eternal Wisdom; the Thought and Substantial Image of God; "He reflects the glory of God and bears the very stamp of his nature" (Heb 1:3). Eternally begotten and eternally loved by the Father, as God from God and Light from Light, he is the principle and archetype of everything created by God in time.

The fact that in the fullness of time the Eternal Word took on the condition of a creature gives a unique *cosmic value* to the event which took place in Bethlehem two thousand years ago. *Thanks to the Word, the world of creatures appears as a "cosmos,"* an ordered universe. And it is the same Word who, *by taking flesh, renews the cosmic order of creation.* The Letter to the Ephesians speaks of the purpose which God had set forth in Christ, "as a plan for the fulness of time, *to unite all things in him,* things in heaven and things on earth" (Eph 1:9-10).

4. Christ, the Redeemer of the world, *is the one Mediator between God and men,* and there is no other name under heaven by which we can be saved (cf. Acts 4:12). As we read in the Letter to the Ephesians: "In him we have redemption through his blood, the forgiveness of our trespasses, according to the richness of his grace, which he has lavished upon us. For he has made known to us in all wisdom and insight... his purpose which he set forth in Christ as a plan for the fulness of time, to unite all things in him, things in heaven and things on earth" (1:7-10). Christ, the Son who is of one being with the Father, is therefore the one who *reveals God's plan for all creation, and for man in particular.* In the memorable phrase of the Second Vatican Council, Christ "fully reveals man to man himself and makes his supreme calling clear."[2] He shows us this calling by revealing the mystery of the Father and His love. As the image of the invisible God, Christ is the perfect man who has restored to the children of Adam the divine likeness which had been deformed by sin. In His human nature, free from all sin and assumed into the divine Person of the Word, the nature shared by all human beings is raised to a sublime dignity: "By his incarnation the Son of God *united himself in some sense with every man.* He labored with human hands, thought with a human mind, acted with a human will and loved with a human heart. Born of Mary the Virgin he truly became one of us and, sin apart, was like us in every way."[3]

5. This "becoming one of us" on the part of the Son of God took place in the greatest humility, so it is no wonder that secular historians, caught up by more stirring events and by famous personages, first made only passing, albeit significant, references to Him. Such references to Christ are found for example in *The Antiquities of the Jews,* a work compiled in Rome between the years 93 and 94 by the historian Flavius Josephus,[4] and especially in the *Annals* of Tacitus, written between the years 115 and 120, where, reporting the burning of Rome in the year 64, falsely attributed by Nero to the Christians, the historian makes an explicit reference to Christ "executed by order of the procurator Pontius Pilate during the reign of Tiberius."[5] Suetonius, too, in his biography of the emperor Claudius, written around 121, informs us that the Jews were expelled from Rome because "under the instigation of a certain Chrestus they stirred up frequent riots."[6] This passage is generally interpreted as referring to Jesus Christ, who had become a source of contention within Jewish circles in Rome. Also of importance as proof of the rapid spread of Christianity is the testimony of Pliny the Younger, the Governor of Bithynia, who reported to the Emperor Trajan, between the years 111 and 113, that a large number of people were accustomed to gather "on a designated day, before dawn, to sing in alternating choirs a hymn to Christ as to a God."[7]

But the great event which non-Christian historians

merely mention in passing takes on its full significance in the writings of the New Testament. These writings, although documents of faith, are no less reliable as historical testimonies, if we consider their references as a whole. Christ, true God and true man, the Lord of the cosmos, is also the Lord of history, of which He is "the Alpha and the Omega" (Rv 1:8; 21:6), "the beginning and the end" (Rv 21:6). In Him the Father has spoken the definitive word about mankind and its history. This is expressed in a concise and powerful way by the Letter to the Hebrews: "In many and various ways God spoke of old to our fathers by the prophets; *but in these last days he has spoken to us by a Son*" (1:1-2).

6. Jesus was born of the Chosen People, in fulfillment of the promise made to Abraham and constantly recalled by the Prophets. The latter spoke in God's name and in his place. The economy of the Old Testament, in fact, was essentially ordered to preparing and proclaiming the coming of Christ, the Redeemer of the universe, and of his Messianic Kingdom. The books of the Old Covenant are thus a permanent witness to a careful divine pedagogy.[8] *In Christ* this pedagogy achieves its purpose: Jesus does not in fact merely speak in the name of God like the Prophets, but he is God Himself speaking in His Eternal Word made flesh. Here we touch upon *the essential point by which Christianity differs from all the other religions,* by which *man's search for God* has been expressed from earliest times. Christianity has its starting point in the Incarnation of the Word. Here it is not simply a case of man seeking God, but of

God who comes in Person to speak to man of Himself and to show him the path by which He may be reached. This is what is proclaimed in the Prologue of John's Gospel: "No one has ever seen God; the only Son, who is in the bosom of the Father, he has made him known" (1:18). *The Incarnate Word is thus the fulfillment of the yearning present in all the religions of mankind:* This fulfillment is brought about by God Himself and transcends all human expectations. It is the mystery of grace.

In Christ, religion is no longer a "blind search for God" (cf. Acts 17:27) but the *response of faith* to God who reveals Himself. It is a response in which man speaks to God as his Creator and Father, a response made possible by that one Man who is also the consubstantial Word in whom God speaks to each individual person and by whom each individual person is enabled to respond to God. What is more, in this Man all creation responds to God. Jesus Christ is the new beginning of everything. In Him all things come into their own; they are taken up and given back to the Creator from whom they first came. *Christ is thus the fulfillment of the yearning of all the world's religions and, as such, He is their sole and definitive completion.* Just as God in Christ speaks to humanity of Himself, so in Christ all humanity and the whole of creation speaks of itself to God—indeed, it gives itself to God. Everything thus returns to its origin. *Jesus Christ is the recapitulation of everything* (cf. Eph 1:10) and at the same time the fulfillment of all things in God: a fulfillment which is the glory of God. The religion founded upon Jesus Christ is a *religion of glory;* it is a newness of life for the praise of the glory of God (cf. Eph 1:12). All creation is in reality a manifestation of His glory. In particular, man (*vivens homo*) is the epiphany of God's glory, man who is called to live by the fullness of life in God.

7. *In Jesus Christ* God not only speaks to man but also *seeks him out*. The Incarnation of the Son of God attests that God goes in search of man. Jesus speaks of this search as the finding of a lost sheep (cf. Lk 15:1-7). It is a search which *begins in the heart of God* and culminates in the Incarnation of the Word. If God goes in search of man, created in His own image and likeness, He does so because He loves him eternally in the Word and wishes to raise him in Christ to the dignity of an adoptive son. God therefore goes in search of man who *is His special possession* in a way unlike any other creature. Man is God's possession by virtue of a choice made in love: God seeks man out, moved by His fatherly heart.

Why does God seek man out? Because man has turned away from Him, hiding himself as Adam did among the trees of the Garden of Eden (cf. Gn 3:8-10). *Man allowed himself to be led astray* by the enemy of God (cf. Gn 3:13). Satan deceived man, persuading him that he too was a god, that he, like God, was capable of knowing good and evil, ruling the world according to his own will without having to take into account the divine will (cf. Gn 3:5). Going in search of man through His Son, God wishes to persuade man to abandon the paths of evil which lead him farther and farther afield. "Making him abandon" those paths means making man understand that he is taking the wrong path; it means *overcoming the evil* which is everywhere found in human history. *Overcoming evil: this is the meaning of the Redemption.* This is brought about in the sacrifice of Christ, by which man redeems the debt of sin and is reconciled to God. The Son of God became man, taking a body and soul in the womb of the Virgin, precisely for this reason: to become the perfect redeeming sacrifice. The religion of the Incarnation is the *religion* of the world's Redemption through the sacrifice of Christ, wherein lies victory over evil, over sin, and over death itself. Accepting death on the Cross, Christ at the same time reveals and gives life because He rises again and death no longer has power over Him.

8. The religion which originates in the mystery of the Redemptive Incarnation is the religion of *"dwelling in the heart of God,"* of sharing in God's very life. St. Paul speaks of this in the passage already quoted: "God has sent the Spirit of his Son into our hearts, crying, 'Abba! Father!'" (Gal 4:6). Man cries out like Christ himself, who turned to God "with loud cries and tears" (Heb 5:7), especially in Gethsemane and on the Cross: man cries out to God just as Christ cried out to Him, and thus he bears witness that he shares in Christ's sonship through the power of the Holy Spirit. The Holy Spirit, whom the Father has sent in the name of the Son, enables man to share in the inmost life of God. He also enables man *to be a son, in the likeness of Christ,* and an heir of all that belongs to the Son (cf. Gal 4:7). In this consists the religion of "dwelling in the inmost life of God," which begins with the Incarnation of the Son of God. The Holy Spirit, who searches the depths of

God (cf. 1 Cor 2:10), leads us, all mankind, into these depths by virtue of the sacrifice of Christ.

II
THE JUBILEE OF THE YEAR 2000

9. Speaking of the birth of the Son of God, St. Paul places this event in the "fullness of time" (cf. Gal 4:4). *Time is indeed fulfilled by the very fact that God, in the Incarnation, came down into human history.* Eternity entered into time: what "fulfillment" could be greater than this? What other "fulfillment" would be possible? Some have thought in terms of certain *mysterious cosmic cycles* in which the history of the universe, and of mankind in particular, would constantly repeat itself. True, man rises from the earth and returns to it (cf. Gen 3:19): this is an immediately evident fact. Yet in man there is an irrepressible longing to live forever. How are we to imagine a life beyond death? Some have considered various forms of *reincarnation:* depending on one's previous life, one would receive a new life in either a higher or lower form until full purification is attained. This belief, deeply rooted in some Eastern religions, itself indicates that man rebels against the finality of death. He is convinced that his nature is essentially spiritual and immortal.

Christian Revelation excludes reincarnation, and speaks of a fulfillment which man is called to achieve in the course of a single earthly existence. Man achieves this fulfillment of his destiny through the sincere gift of self, a gift which is made possible only through his encounter with God. It is in God that man finds his full self-realization: *this is the truth revealed by Christ.* Man fulfills himself in God, who comes to meet him through his Eternal Son. Thanks to God's coming on earth, human time, which began at Creation, has reached its fullness. "The fullness of time" is in fact eternity, indeed, it is *the One who is eternal,* God Himself. Thus, to enter into "the fullness of time" means to reach the end of time and to transcend its limits, in order to find time's fulfillment in the eternity of God.

10. *In Christianity time has a fundamental importance.* Within the dimension of time the world was created; within it the history of salvation unfolds, finding its culmination in the "fullness of time" of the Incarnation and its goal in the glorious return of the Son of God at the end of time. *In Jesus Christ, the Word made flesh, time becomes a dimension of God,* who is Himself eternal. With the coming of Christ there begin "the last days" (cf. Heb 1:2), the "last hour" (cf. 1 Jn 2:18), and the time of the Church, which will last until the Parousia.

From this relationship of God with time there arises *the duty to sanctify time.* This is done, for example, when individual times, days, or weeks are dedicated to God, as once happened in the religion of the Old Covenant, and as happens still, though in a new way, in Christianity. In the liturgy of the Easter Vigil the celebrant, as he blesses the candle which symbolizes the risen Christ, proclaims: "Christ yesterday and today, the beginning and the end, Alpha and Omega, all time belongs to him, and all the ages, to him be glory and power through every age for ever."

He says these words as he inscribes on the candle the numerals of the current year. The meaning of this rite is clear: It emphasizes the fact that *Christ is the Lord of time;* He is its beginning and its end; every year, every day, and every moment are embraced by his Incarnation and Resurrection, and thus become part of the "fullness of time." For this reason, the Church too lives and celebrates the liturgy in the span of a year. *The solar year is thus permeated by the liturgical year,* which in a certain way reproduces the whole mystery of the Incarnation and Redemption, beginning from the first Sunday of Advent and ending on the Solemnity of Christ the King, Lord of the Universe and Lord of History. Every Sunday commemorates the day of the Lord's Resurrection.

11. Against this background we can understand *the Custom of Jubilees,* which began in the Old Testament and continues in the history of the Church. Jesus of Nazareth, going back one day to the *synagogue of his hometown,* stood up to read (cf. Lk 4:16-30). Taking the book of the Prophet Isaiah, he read this passage: "The Spirit of the Lord God is upon me, because the Lord has anointed me to bring good tidings to the afflicted; he has sent me to bind up the brokenhearted, to proclaim liberty to the captives, and the opening of the prison to those who are bound; *to proclaim the year of the Lord's favor"* (61:1-2).

The Prophet was speaking of the Messiah. "Today," Jesus added, "this scripture has been fulfilled in your hearing" (Lk 4:21), thus indicating that He Himself was the Messiah foretold by the prophet, and that the long-expected "time" was beginning in

Him. The day of salvation had come, the "fullness of time." *All Jubilees point to this "time" and refer to the Messianic mission of Christ,* who came as the one "anointed" by the Holy Spirit, the one "sent by the Father." It is He who proclaims the good news to the poor. It is He who brings liberty to those deprived of it, who frees the oppressed and gives back sight to the blind (cf. Mt 11:4-5; Lk 7:22). In this way He ushers in "a year of the Lord's favor," which He proclaims not only with His words but above all by His actions. The Jubilee, "a year of the Lord's favor," characterizes all the activity of Jesus; it is not merely the recurrence of an anniversary in time.

12. *The words and deeds of Jesus thus represent the fulfillment of the whole tradition of Jubilees* in the Old Testament. We know that the Jubilee was *a time dedicated in a special way to God.* It fell every seventh year, according to the Law of Moses: this was the "sabbatical year," during which the earth was left fallow and slaves were set free. The duty to free slaves was regulated by detailed prescriptions contained in the Books of Exodus (23:10-11), Leviticus (25:1-28), and Deuteronomy (15:1-6). In other words, these prescriptions are found in practically the whole of biblical legislation, which is thus marked by this very specific characteristic. In the sabbatical year, in addition to the freeing of slaves the Law also provided for the cancellation of all debts in accordance with precise regulations. And all this was to be done in honor of God. What was true for the sabbatical year was also true for the *Jubilee* year, which fell every fifty years. In the jubilee year, however, the customs of the sabbatical year were broadened and celebrated with even greater solemnity. As we read in Leviticus: "You shall hallow the 50th year and proclaim liberty throughout the land to all its inhabitants; it shall be a jubilee for you, when each of you shall return to his property and each of you shall return to his family" (25:10). One of the most significant consequences of the Jubilee year was the general *"emancipation" of all the dwellers on the land in need of being freed.* On this occasion every Israelite regained possession of his ancestral land, if he happened to have sold it or lost it by falling into slavery. He could never be completely deprived of the land, because it belonged to God; nor could the Israelites remain forever in a state of slavery, since God had "redeemed" them for Himself as His exclusive possession by freeing them from slavery in Egypt.

13. The prescriptions for the Jubilee year largely remained ideals—more a hope than an actual fact. They thus became a *prophetia futuri* insofar as they foretold the freedom which would be won by the coming Messiah. Even so, on the basis of the juridical norms contained in these prescriptions a kind of *social doctrine* began to emerge, which would then more clearly develop beginning with the New Testament. *The Jubilee year was meant to restore equality among all the children of Israel,* offering new possibilities to families which had lost their property and even their personal freedom. On the other hand, the Jubilee year was a reminder to the rich that a time would come when their Israelite slaves would once again become their equals and would be able to reclaim their rights. At the times prescribed by Law, a Jubilee year had to be proclaimed, to assist those in need. This was required by just government. *Justice, according to the Law of Israel, consisted above all in the protection of the weak,* and a king was supposed to be outstanding in this regard, as the psalmist says: "He delivers the needy when he calls, the poor and him who has no helper. He has pity on the weak and the needy, and saves the lives of the needy" (Ps 72:12-13). *The foundations of this tradition were strictly theological,* linked first of all with the theology of Creation and with that of Divine Providence. It was a common conviction, in fact, that *to God alone, as Creator, belonged the "dominium altum"*—lordship over all creation and over the earth in particular (cf. Lv 25:23). If in His Providence God had given the earth to humanity, that meant that He had given it to everyone. Therefore *the riches of Creation were to be considered as a common good of the whole of humanity.* Those who possessed these goods as personal property were really only stewards, ministers charged with working in the name of God, who remains the sole owner in the full sense, since it is God's will that created goods should serve everyone in a just way. *The Jubilee year was meant to restore this social justice.* The social doctrine of the Church, which has always been a part of Church teaching and which has developed greatly in the last century, particularly after the encyclical *Rerum Novarum,* is rooted in the tradition of the Jubilee year.

14. What needs to be emphasized, however, is what Isaiah expresses in the words *"to proclaim the year of the Lord's favor."* For the Church, the Jubilee is precisely this "year of the Lord's favor," a year of the remission of sins and of the punishments due to them, a year of reconciliation between disputing parties, a year of manifold conversions and of sacramental and extra-sacramental penance. The tradition of Jubilee years involves the *granting* of indulgences on a larger scale than at other times. Together with Jubilees recalling the mystery of the Incarnation, at intervals of one hundred, fifty, and twenty-five years, there are also Jubilees which commemorate the event of the Redemption: the Cross of Christ, his death on Golgotha, and the Resurrection. On these occasions, the Church proclaims "a year of the Lord's favor," and she tries to ensure that all the faithful can bene-fit from this grace. *That is why Jubilees are celebrated not only "in Urbe" but also "extra Urbem":* traditionally the latter took place the year after the celebration "in Urbe."

15. *In the lives of individuals, Jubilees* are usually con-nected with the date of birth; but other anniversaries are also celebrated such as those of Baptism, Con-firmation, First Communion, Priestly or Episcopal Ordination, and the Sacrament of Marriage. Some of these anniversaries have parallels in the secular world, but Christians always give them a religious character. In fact, in the Christian view every Jubilee—the 25th of Marriage or Priesthood, known as "silver," the 50th, known as "golden," or the 60th, known as "diamond"—is a *particular year of favor* for the individual who has received one or other of the Sacraments. What we have said about individuals with regard to Jubilees can also be applied to *communities* *or institutions.* Thus we celebrate the centenary or the millennium of the foundation of a town or city. In the Church, we celebrate the Jubilees of parishes and dioceses. All these personal and community Jubilees have an important and significant role in the lives of individuals and communities.

In view of this, *the two thousand years which have passed since the birth of Christ* (prescinding from the question of its precise chronology) *represent an extraordinarily great Jubilee,* not only for Christians but indirectly for the whole of humanity, given the prominent role played by Christianity during these two millennia. It is significant that the calculation of the passing years begins almost everywhere with the year of Christ's coming into the world, which is thus *the center* of the calendar most widely used today. Is this not another sign of the unparalleled effect of the birth of Jesus of Nazareth on the history of mankind?

16. *The term "Jubilee" speaks of joy;* not just an inner joy but a jubilation which is manifested outwardly, for the coming of God is also an outward, visible, audible, and tangible event, as St. John makes clear (cf. 1 Jn 1:1). It is thus appropriate that every sign of joy at this coming should have its own outward expression. This will demonstrate that *the Church rejoices in salvation.* She invites everyone to rejoice, and she tries to create conditions to ensure that the power of salvation may be shared by all. Hence the Year 2000 will be celebrated as the Great Jubilee.

With regard to its *content, this Great Jubilee* will be, in a certain sense, like any other. But at the same time it will be different, greater than any other. For the Church respects the measurements of time: hours, days, years, centuries. She thus goes forward with every individual, helping everyone to realize how *each of these measurements of time is imbued with the presence of God* and with His saving activity. In this spirit the Church rejoices, gives thanks, and asks forgiveness, presenting her petitions to the Lord of history and of human consciences.

Among the most fervent petitions which the Church makes to the Lord during this important time, as the eve of the new millennium approaches, is that unity among all Christians of the various confessions will increase until they reach full communion. I pray that the Jubilee will be a promising opportunity for fruitful cooperation in the many areas which unite us; these are unquestionably more numerous than those which divide us. It would thus be quite helpful if, with due respect for the programs of the individual churches and communities, ecumenical agreements could be reached with regard to the preparation and celebration of the Jubilee. In this way the Jubilee will bear witness even more forcefully before the world that the disciples of Christ are fully resolved to reach full unity as soon as possible in the certainty that "nothing is impossible with God."

III
PREPARATION FOR THE GREAT JUBILEE

17. *In the Church's history every Jubilee is prepared for by Divine Providence.* This is true also of the Great Jubilee of the Year 2000. With this conviction, we look today with a sense of gratitude and yet with a sense of responsibility at all that has happened in human history since the birth of Christ, particularly the events which have occurred between the years 1000 and 2000. But in a very particular way, we look with the eyes of faith to our own century, searching out whatever bears witness not only to man's history but also to God's intervention in human affairs.

18. From this point of view we can affirm that *the Second Vatican Council was a providential event whereby the Church began the more immediate preparation* for the Jubilee of the second millennium. It was a Council similar to earlier ones, yet very different; it was a Council *focused on the mystery of Christ and his Church, and at the same time open to the world.* This openness was an evangelical response to recent changes in the world, including the profoundly disturbing experiences of the twentieth century, a century scarred by the First and Second World Wars, by the experience of concentration camps, and by horrendous massacres. All these events demonstrate most vividly that the world needs purification; it needs to be converted.

The Second Vatican Council is often considered as the beginning of a new era in the life of the Church. This is true, but at the same time it is difficult to overlook the fact that *the Council drew much from the experiences and reflections of the immediate past,* especially from the intellectual legacy left by Pius XII. In the history of the Church, the "old" and the "new" are always closely interwoven. The "new" grows out of the "old," and the "old" finds a fuller expression in the "new." Thus it was for the Second Vatican Council and for the activity of the popes connected with the Council, starting with John XXIII, continuing with Paul VI and John Paul I, up to the present pope.

What these popes have accomplished during and since the Council, in their Magisterium no less than in their pastoral activity, has certainly made a significant contribution to the *preparation of that new springtime of Christian life* which will be revealed by the Great Jubilee, if Christians are docile to the action of the Holy Spirit.

19. The Council, while not imitating the sternness of John the Baptist, who called for repentance and conversion on the banks of the Jordan (cf. Lk 3:1-7), did show something of the Prophet of old, pointing out with fresh vigor to the men and women of today that Jesus Christ is the "Lamb of God who takes away the sin of the world" (Jn 1:29), the Redeemer of humanity, and the Lord of history. During the Council, precisely out of a desire to be fully faithful to her Master, the Church questioned herself about her own identity and discovered anew the depth of her mystery as the Body and the Bride of Christ. Humbly heeding the Word of God, she reaffirmed the universal call to holiness; she made provision for the reform of the liturgy, the "origin and summit" of her life; she gave impetus to the renewal of many aspects of her life at the universal level and in the local churches; she strove to promote the various Christian vocations, from those of the laity to those of religious, from the ministry of deacons to that of priests and bishops; and in a particular way she rediscovered episcopal collegiality, that privileged expression of the pastoral service carried out by the bishops in communion with the successor of Peter. On the basis of this profound renewal, the Council opened itself to Christians of other denominations, to the followers of other religions, and to all the people of our time. No council had ever spoken so clearly about Christian unity, about dialogue with non-Christian religions, about the specific meaning of the Old Covenant and of Israel, about the dignity of each person's conscience, about the principle of religious liberty, about the different cultural traditions within which the Church carries out her missionary mandate, and about the means of social communication.

20. The Council's enormously rich body of teaching and *the striking new tone* in the way it presented this content constitute as it were a proclamation of new times. The Council Fathers spoke in the language of the Gospel, the language of the Sermon on the Mount and the Beatitudes. In the Council's message God is presented *in his absolute lordship over all things,* but also as *the One who ensures the authentic autonomy of earthly realities.*

The best preparation for the new millennium, therefore, can only be expressed in a renewed commitment *to apply,* as faithfully as possible, *the teachings of Vatican II to the life of every individual and of the whole Church.* It was with the Second Vatican Council that, in the broadest sense of the term, the immediate preparations for the Great Jubilee of the Year 2000 were really begun. If we look for an analogy in the liturgy, it could be said that the yearly *Advent liturgy* is the season nearest to the spirit of the Council. For

Advent prepares us to meet the One who was, who is, and who is to come (cf. Rv 4:8).

21. Part of the preparation for the approach of the year 2000 is the *series of Synods* begun after the Second Vatican Council: general Synods together with continental, regional, national and diocesan Synods. The theme underlying them all is *evangelization,* or rather the new evangelization, the foundations of which were laid down in the Apostolic Exhortation *Evangelii Nuntiandi* of Pope Paul VI, issued in 1975 following the Third General Assembly of the Synod of Bishops. These Synods themselves are part of the new evangelization: they were born of the Second Vatican Council's vision of the Church. They open up broad areas for the participation of the laity, whose specific responsibilities in the Church they define. They are an expression of the strength which Christ has given to the entire People of God, making it a sharer in His own Messianic mission as Prophet, Priest, and King. Very eloquent in this regard are the statements of the Dogmatic Constitution *Lumen Gentium. The preparation for the Jubilee year 2000 is thus taking place throughout the whole Church, on the universal and local levels,* giving her a new awareness of the salvific mission she has received from Christ. This awareness is particularly evident in the Post-Synodal Exhortations devoted to the mission of the laity, the formation of priests, catechesis, the family, the value of penance and reconciliation in the life of the Church and of humanity in general, as well as in the forthcoming one to be devoted to the consecrated life.

22. Special tasks and responsibilities with regard to the Great Jubilee of the year 2000 belong to the *ministry of the Bishop of Rome*. In a certain sense, all the popes of the past century have prepared for this Jubilee. With his program to renew all things in Christ, St. Pius X tried to forestall the tragic developments which arose from the international situation at the beginning of this century. The Church was aware of her duty to act decisively to promote and defend the basic values of peace and justice in the face of contrary tendencies in our time. The Popes of the period before the Council acted with firm commitment, each in his own way: Benedict XV found himself faced with the tragedy of the First World War; Pius XI had to contend with the threats of totalitarian systems or systems which did not respect human freedom in Germany, in Russia, in Italy, in Spain, and even earlier still in Mexico. Pius XII took steps to counter the very grave injustice brought about by a total contempt for human dignity at the time of the Second World War. He also provided enlightened guidelines for the birth of a new world order after the fall of the previous political systems.

Furthermore, in the course of this century the Popes, following in the footsteps of Leo XIII, systematically developed the themes of Catholic social doctrine, expounding the characteristics of a *just system* in the area of relations between labor and capital. We may recall the encyclical *Quadragesimo Anno* of Pius XI, the numerous interventions of Pius XII, the encyclicals *Mater et Magistra* and *Pacem in Terris* of John XXIII, the Encyclical *Populorum Progressio* and the apostolic letter *Octogesima Adveniens* of Paul VI. I too have frequently dealt with this subject. I specifically devoted the encyclical *Laborem Exercens* to the importance of human labor, while in *Centesimus Annus* I wished to reaffirm the relevance, one hundred years later, of the doctrine presented in *Rerum Novarum*. In my encyclical *Sollicitudo Rei Socialis* I had earlier offered a systematic reformulation of the Church's entire social doctrine against the background of the East-West confrontation and the danger of nuclear war. The two elements of the Church's social doctrine—the *safeguarding of human dignity and rights* in the sphere of a just relation between labor and capital, and *the promotion of peace*—were closely joined in this text. The papal messages of 1 January each year, begun in 1968 in the pontificate of Paul VI, are also meant to serve the cause of peace.

23. Since the publication of the very first document of my Pontificate, *I have spoken explicitly of the Great Jubilee,* suggesting that the time leading up to it be lived as "a new Advent."[9] This theme has since reappeared many times, and was dwelt upon at length in the encyclical *Dominum et Vivificantem.*[10] In fact, preparing for the *year 2000 has become as it were a hermeneutical key of my Pontificate*. It is certainly not a matter of indulging in a new millenarianism, as occurred in some quarters at the end of the first millennium; rather, it is *aimed at an increased sensitivity to all that the Spirit is saying to the Church and to the churches* (cf. Rv 2:7 ff.), as well as to individuals through charisms meant to serve the whole community. The purpose is to emphasize what the Spirit is suggesting to the different communities, from the smallest ones, such as the family, to the largest ones, such as nations and international organizations, taking into account cultures, societies, and sound traditions. Despite appearances, humanity continues to await the revelation of the children of God and lives by this hope, like a mother in labor, to use the image employed so powerfully by St. Paul in his Letter to the Romans (cf. 8:19-22).

24. *Papal journeys* have become an important element in the work of implementing the Second Vatican Council. Begun by John XXIII on the eve of the Council with a memorable pilgrimage to Loreto and Assisi (1962), they notably increased under Paul VI, who after first visiting the Holy Land (1964) undertook nine other great apostolic journeys which brought him into direct contact with the peoples of the different continents.

The current Pontificate has widened this program of travels even further, starting with Mexico, on the occasion of the Third General Conference of the Latin American Episcopate held in Puebla in 1979. In that same year there was also the trip to Poland for the Jubilee of the nine hundredth anniversary of the death of St. Stanislaus, bishop and martyr.

The successive stages of these travels are well known. Papal journeys have become a regular occurrence, taking in the particular churches in every continent and showing concern *for the development of ecumenical relationships* with Christians of various denominations. Particularly important in this regard were the visits to Turkey (1979), Germany (1980), England, Scotland, and Wales (1982),

Switzerland (1984), the Scandinavian countries (1989), and most recently the Baltic countries (1993).

At present, it is my fervent wish to visit Sarajevo in Bosnia-Herzegovina and the Middle East: Lebanon, Jerusalem, and the Holy Land. It would be very significant if in the year 2000 it were possible to visit the *places on the road taken by the People of God of the Old Covenant,* starting from the places associated with Abraham and Moses, through Egypt and Mount Sinai, as far as Damascus, the city which witnessed the conversion of St. Paul.

25. In preparing for the year 2000, *the individual churches* have their own role to play, as they celebrate with their own Jubilees significant stages in the salvation history of the various peoples. Among these regional or *local Jubilees,* events of great importance have included the millennium of the Baptism of Rus' in 1988[11] as also the five hundredth anniversary of the beginning of evangelization in America (1492). Besides events of such wide-ranging impact, we may recall others which, although not of universal importance, are no less significant: for example, the millennium of the Baptism of Poland in 1966 and of the Baptism of Hungary in 1968, together with the six hundredth anniversary of the Baptism of Lithuania in 1987. There will soon also be celebrated the fifteen hundredth anniversary of the baptism of Clovis (496), King of the Franks, and the fourteen hundredth anniversary of the arrival of St. Augustine in Canterbury (597), marking the beginning of the evangelization of the Anglo-Saxon world.

As far as Asia is concerned, the Jubilee will remind

us of the Apostle Thomas, who, according to tradition, brought the proclamation of the Gospel at the very beginning of the Christian era to India, where missionaries from Portugal would not arrive until about the year 1500. The current year also marks the seventh centenary of the evangelization of China (1294), and we are preparing to commemorate the spread of missionary work in the Philippines with the erection of the Metropolitan See of Manila (1595). We likewise look forward to the fourth centenary of the first martyrs in Japan (1597).

In Africa, where the first proclamation of the Gospel also dates back to apostolic times, together with the 1,650th anniversary of the episcopal consecration of the first bishop of the Ethiopians, St. Frumentius (c. 340), and the five hundredth anniversary of the beginning of the evangelization of Angola in the ancient Kingdom of the Congo (1491), nations such as Cameroon, Côte d'Ivoire, the Central African Republic, Burundi and Burkina Faso are celebrating the centenaries of the arrival of the first missionaries in their respective territories. Other African nations have recently celebrated such centenaries.

And how can we fail to mention the Eastern Churches, whose ancient Patriarchates are so closely linked to the apostolic heritage and whose venerable theological, liturgical, and spiritual traditions constitute a tremendous wealth which is the common patrimony of the whole of Christianity? The many Jubilee celebrations in these churches and in the communities which acknowledge them as the origin of their own apostolicity recall the journey of Christ down the centuries, leading to the Great Jubilee at the end of the second millennium.

Seen in this light, the whole of Christian history appears to us as a single river, into which many tributaries pour their waters. The year 2000 invites us to gather with renewed fidelity and ever deeper communion *along the banks of this great river:* the river of Revelation, of Christianity, and of the Church, a river which flows through human history starting from the event which took place at Nazareth and then at Bethlehem two thousand years ago. This is truly the "river" which with its "streams," in the expression of the psalm, "make glad the city of God" (46:4).

26. The *Holy Years* celebrated in the latter part of this century have also prepared for the year 2000. *The Holy Year* proclaimed by Paul VI in *1975* is still fresh in our memory. The celebration of *1983* as *the Year of Redemption* followed along the same lines. *The Marian Year 1986/87* perhaps struck a more resounding chord; it was eagerly awaited and profoundly experienced in the individual local churches, especially at the Marian shrines around the world. The encyclical *Redemptoris Mater,* issued on that occasion, drew attention to the Council's teaching on the presence of the Mother of God in the mystery of Christ and the Church: two thousand years ago the Son of God was made man by the power of the Holy Spirit and was born of the Immaculate Virgin Mary. *The Marian Year was as it were an anticipation of the Jubilee,* and contained much of what will find fuller expression in the year 2000.

27. It would be difficult not to recall that the Marian Year took place only shortly before *the events of 1989.* Those events remain surprising for their vastness and especially for the speed with which they occurred. The '80s were years marked by a growing danger from the "Cold War." 1989 ushered in a peaceful resolution which took the form, as it were, of an "organic" development. In the light of this fact, we are led to recognize a truly prophetic significance in the encyclical *Rerum Novarum:* everything that Pope Leo XIII wrote there about Communism was borne out by these events, as I emphasized in the encyclical *Centesimus Annus.*[12] In the unfolding of those events one could already discern the invisible hand of Providence at work with maternal care: "Can a woman forget her infant?" (cf. Is 49:15).

After 1989 however there arose *new dangers and threats.* In the countries of the former Eastern bloc, after the fall of Communism, there appeared the serious threat of exaggerated nationalism, as is evident from events in the Balkans and other neighboring areas. This obliges the European nations to make a serious *examination of conscience* and to acknowledge faults and errors, both economic and political, resulting from imperialist policies carried out in the previous and present centuries vis-à-vis nations whose rights have been systematically violated.

28. In the wake of the Marian Year, we are now observing *the Year of the Family,* a celebration which is closely connected with the mystery of the Incarnation and with the very history of humanity. Thus there is good cause to hope that the Year of the

Family, inaugurated at Nazareth, will become, like the Marian Year, *another significant stage in preparation for the Great Jubilee.*

With this in view, I wrote a *Letter to Families,* the purpose of which was to restate the substance of the Church's teaching on the family and to bring this teaching, so to speak, into every home. At the Second Vatican Council, the Church recognized her duty to promote the dignity of marriage and the family.[13] The Year of the Family is meant to help make the Council's teaching in this regard a reality. *Each family, in some way, should be involved in the preparation for the Great Jubilee.* Was it not through a family, the family of Nazareth, that the Son of God chose to enter into human history?

IV
IMMEDIATE PREPARATION

29. Against the background of this sweeping panorama a question arises: Can we draw up *a specific program* of initiatives for the *immediate preparation* of the Great Jubilee? In fact, what has been said above already includes some elements of such a program.

A more detailed plan of specific events will call for widespread consultation in order for it not to be artificial and difficult to implement in the particular churches, which live in such different conditions. For this reason I wished to consult the Presidents of the Episcopal Conferences and especially the Cardinals.

I am grateful to the members of the College of Cardinals who met in Extraordinary Consistory on 13-14 June 1994, considered numerous proposals, and suggested helpful guidelines. I also thank my brothers in the Episcopate who in various ways communicated valuable ideas, which I have kept carefully in mind while writing this apostolic letter.

30. The first recommendation which clearly emerged from the consultation regards *the period of preparation.* Only a few years now separate us from the year 2000: it seemed fitting to divide this period into *two phases,* reserving the *strictly preparatory* phase for the last three years. It was thought that the accumulation of many activities over the course of a longer period of preparation would detract from its spiritual intensity.

It was therefore considered appropriate to approach the historic date with a *first phase,* which would make the faithful aware of general themes, and then to concentrate the direct and immediate preparation into a *second phase* consisting of a *three-year period* wholly directed to the celebration of the mystery of Christ the Savior.

A) First Phase

31. *The first phase* will therefore be of an *ante-preparatory* character; it is meant to revive in the Christian people an awareness of the value and meaning of the Jubilee of the year 2000 *in human history.* As a commemoration of the birth of Christ, the Jubilee is *deeply charged with Christological significance.*

In keeping with the unfolding of the Christian faith in word and sacrament, it seems important, even in this special anniversary, to link the structure of *memorial* with that of *celebration,* not limiting commemoration of the event only to ideas but also making its saving significance present through the celebration of the sacraments. The Jubilee celebration should confirm the Christians of today in their *faith* in God who has revealed himself in Christ, sustain their *hope* which reaches out in expectation of eternal life, and rekindle their *charity* in active service to their brothers and sisters.

During the first stage (1994 to 1996) the Holy See, through a special *Committee* established for this purpose, will suggest courses of reflection and action at the universal level. A similar commitment to promoting awareness will be carried out in a more detailed way by corresponding *commissions in the local churches.* In a way, it is a question of continuing what was done in the period of remote preparation and at the same time of *coming to a deeper appreciation of the most significant aspects of the Jubilee celebration.*

32. A Jubilee is always an occasion of special grace, "a day blessed by the Lord." As has already been noted, it is thus a time of joy. The Jubilee of the year 2000 is meant to be a great *prayer of praise and thanksgiving,* especially for the *gift of the Incarnation of the Son of God and of the Redemption* which He accomplished. In the Jubilee year Christians will stand with the renewed wonder of faith before the love of the Father, who *gave His Son,* "that whoever believes in him should not perish but have eternal life" (Jn 3:16). With a profound sense of commitment, they will likewise express their gratitude for the *gift of the Church,* established by Christ as "a kind of sacrament or sign of intimate union with God, and of the unity of all mankind."[14] Their thanksgiving will embrace the *fruits of holiness* which have matured in the life of all those many men and women who in every generation and every period of history have fully welcomed the gift of Redemption.

Nevertheless, the joy of every Jubilee is above all a *joy based upon the forgiveness of sins, the joy of conversion.* It therefore seems appropriate to emphasize once more the theme of the *Synod of Bishops in 1984: penance and reconciliation.*[15] That synod was an event of extraordinary significance in the life of the postconciliar Church. It took up the ever topical question of conversion (*metanoia*), which is the precondition for reconciliation with God on the part of both individuals and communities.

33. Hence it is appropriate that, as the second millennium of Christianity draws to a close, the Church should become more fully conscious of the sinfulness of her children, recalling all those times in history when they departed from the spirit of Christ and his Gospel and, instead of offering to the world the witness of a life inspired by the values of faith, indulged in ways of thinking and acting which were truly *forms of counter-witness and scandal.*

Although she is holy because of her incorporation into Christ, the Church does not tire of doing penance: Before God and man *she always acknowledges as her own her sinful sons and daughters.* As *Lumen Gentium* affirms: "The Church, embracing sinners to her bosom, is at the same time holy and always in need of being purified, and incessantly pursues the path of penance and renewal."[16]

The Holy Door of the Jubilee of the year 2000 should be symbolically wider than those of previous Jubilees, because humanity, upon reaching this goal, will leave behind not just a century but a millennium. It is fitting that the Church should make this passage with a clear awareness of what has happened to her during the last ten centuries. She cannot cross the threshold of the new millennium without encouraging her children to purify themselves, through repentance, of past errors and instances of infidelity, inconsistency, and slowness to act. Acknowledging the weaknesses of the past is an act of honesty and courage which helps us to strengthen our faith, which alerts us to face today's temptations and challenges and prepares us to meet them.

34. Among the sins which require a greater commitment to repentance and conversion should certainly be counted those which *have been detrimental to the unity willed by God for His People.* In the course of the thousand years now drawing to a close, even more than in the first millennium, ecclesial communion has been painfully wounded, a fact "for which, at times, men of both sides were to blame."[17] Such wounds openly contradict the will of Christ and are a cause of scandal to the world.[18] These sins of the past unfortunately still burden us and remain ever present temptations. It is necessary to make amends for them, and earnestly to beseech Christ's forgiveness.

In these last years of the millennium, the Church should invoke the Holy Spirit with ever greater insistence, imploring from Him the grace of *Christian unity.* This is a crucial matter for our testimony to the

Gospel before the world. Especially since the Second Vatican Council many ecumenical initiatives have been undertaken with generosity and commitment: it can be said that the whole activity of the local churches and of the Apostolic See has taken on an ecumenical dimension in recent years. The *Pontifical Council for the Promotion of Christian Unity* has become an important catalyst in the movement toward full unity.

We are all however aware that the attainment of this goal cannot be the fruit of human efforts alone, vital though they are. *Unity, after all, is a gift of the Holy Spirit.* We are asked to respond to this gift responsibly, without compromise in our witness to the truth, generously implementing the guidelines laid down by the Council and in subsequent documents of the Holy See, which are also highly regarded by many Christians not in full communion with the Catholic Church.

This then is one of the tasks of Christians as we make our way to the year 2000. The approaching end of the second millennium demands of everyone an *examination of conscience* and the promotion of fitting ecumenical initiatives, so that we can celebrate the Great Jubilee, if not completely united, *at least much closer to overcoming the divisions of the second millen-nium.* As everyone recognizes, an enormous effort is needed in this regard. It is essential not only to continue along the path of dialogue on doctrinal matters, but above all to be more committed to *prayer for Christian unity.* Such prayer has become much more intense after the Council, but it must increase still more, involving an ever greater number of Christians, in unison with the great petition of Christ before his Passion: "Father... that they also may all be one in us" (cf. Jn 17:21).

35. Another painful chapter of history to which the sons and daughters of the Church must return with a spirit of repentance is that of the acquiescence given, especially in certain centuries, to *intolerance and even the use of violence* in the service of truth.

It is true that an accurate historical judgment cannot prescind from careful study of the cultural conditioning of the times, as a result of which many people may have held in good faith that an authentic witness to the truth could include suppressing the opinions of others or at least paying no attention to them. Many factors frequently converged to create assumptions which justified intolerance and fostered an emotional climate from which only great spirits, truly free and filled with God, were in some way able to break free. Yet the consideration of mitigating factors does not exonerate the Church from the obligation to express profound regret for the weaknesses of so many of her sons and daughters who sullied her face, preventing her from fully mirroring the image of her crucified Lord, the supreme witness of patient love and of humble meekness. From these painful moments of the past a lesson can be drawn for the future, leading all Christians to adhere fully to the sublime principle stated by the Council: "The truth cannot impose itself except by virtue of its own truth, as it wins over the mind with both gentleness and power."[19]

36. Many cardinals and bishops expressed the desire for a serious examination of conscience above all on the part of *the Church of today*. On the threshold of the new millennium Christians need to place themselves humbly before the Lord and examine themselves on *the responsibility which they too have for the evils of our day*. The present age in fact, together with much light, also presents not a few shadows.

How can we remain silent, for example, about the *religious indifference* which causes many people today to live as if God did not exist or to be content with a vague religiosity, incapable of coming to grips with the question of truth and the requirement of consistency? To this must also be added the widespread loss of the transcendent sense of human life and confusion in the ethical sphere, even about the fundamental values of respect for life and the family. The sons and daughters of the Church, too, need to examine themselves in this regard. To what extent have they been shaped by the climate of secularism and ethical relativism? And what responsibility do they bear, in view of the increasing lack of religion, for not having shown the true face of God, by having "failed in their religious, moral or social life"?[20]

It cannot be denied that for many Christians the spiritual life is passing through *a time of uncertainty* which affects not only their moral life but also their life of prayer and the *theological correctness of their faith*. Faith, already put to the test by the challenges of our times, is sometimes disoriented by erroneous theological views, the spread of which is abetted by the crisis of obedience vis-à-vis the Church's Magisterium.

And with respect to the Church of our time, how can we not lament *the lack of discernment,* which at times became even acquiescence, shown by many Christians concerning the violation of fundamental human rights by totalitarian regimes? And should we not also regret, among the shadows of our own day, the responsibility shared by so many Christians *for grave forms of injustice and exclusion?* It must be asked how many Christians really know and put into practice the principles of the Church's social doctrine.

An examination of conscience must also consider *the reception given to the Council,* this great gift of the Spirit to the Church at the end of the second millennium. To what extent has the Word of God become more fully the soul of theology and the inspiration of the whole of Christian living, as *Dei Verbum* sought? Is the liturgy lived as the "origin and summit" of ecclesial life, in accordance with the teaching of *Sacrosanctum Concilium?* In the universal Church and in the particular churches, is the ecclesiology of communion described in *Lumen Gentium* being strengthened? Does it leave room for charisms, ministries, and different forms of participation by the People of God, without adopting notions borrowed from democracy and sociology which do not reflect the Catholic vision of the Church and the authentic spirit of Vatican II? Another serious question is raised by the nature of relations between the Church and the world. The Council's guidelines—set forth in *Guadium et Spes* and other documents—of open, respectful, and cordial dialogue, yet accompanied by careful discernment and courageous witness to the truth, remain valid and call us to a greater commitment.

37. The Church of the first millennium was born of the blood of the martyrs: *"Sanguis martyrum—semen christianorum."*[21] The historical events linked to the figure of Constantine the Great could never have ensured the development of the Church as it occurred during the first millennium if it had not been for the *seeds sown by the martyrs and the heritage of sanctity which marked the first Christian generations.* At the end of the second millennium, *the Church has once again become a Church of martyrs.* The persecutions of believers—priests, religious, and laity—has caused a great sowing of martyrdom in different parts of the world. The witness to Christ borne even to the shedding of blood has become a common inheritance of Catholics, Orthodox, Anglicans, and Protestants, as Pope Paul VI pointed out in his homily for the canonization of the Ugandan martyrs.[22]

This witness must not be forgotten. The Church of the first centuries, although facing considerable organizational difficulties, took care to write down in special martyrologies. Theses martyrologies have been constantly updated through the centuries, and the register of the saints and the blessed bears the names not only of those who have shed their blood for Christ but also of teachers of the faith, missionaries, confessors, bishops, priests, virgins, married couples, widows, and children.

In our own century the martyrs have returned, many of them nameless, *"unknown soldiers"* as it were *of God's great cause.* As far as possible, their witness should not be lost to the Church. As was recommended in the Consistory, *the local churches should do everything possible to ensure that the memory of those who have suffered martyrdom should be safeguarded, gathering the necessary documentation.* This gesture cannot fail to have an ecumenical character and expression. Perhaps the most convincing form of ecumenism is *the ecumenism of the saints* and of the martyrs. The *communio sanctorum* speaks louder than the things which divide us. The *martyrologium* of the first centuries was the basis of the veneration of the saints. By proclaiming and venerating the holiness of her sons and daughters, the Church gave supreme honor to God Himself; in the martyrs she venerated Christ, who was at the origin of their martyrdom and of their holiness. In later times there developed the practice of canonization, a practice which still continues in the Catholic Church and in the Orthodox Churches. In recent years the number of canonizations and beatifications has increased. These show *the vitality of the local churches,* which are much more numerous today than in the first centuries and in the first millennium. The greatest homage which all the churches can give to Christ on the threshold of the third millennium will be to manifest the Redeemer's all-powerful presence through the fruits of faith, hope, and charity present in men and women of many different tongues and races who have followed Christ in the various forms of the Christian vocation.

It will be the task of the Apostolic See, in preparation for the year 2000, *to update the martyrologies* for the universal Church, paying careful attention to the holiness of those who *in our own time* lived fully by the truth of Christ. In particular, there is a need to foster the recognition of the heroic virtues of men and women who have lived their Christian vocation *in marriage.* Precisely because we are convinced of the abundant fruits of holiness in the married state, we need to find the most appropriate means for discerning them and proposing them to the whole Church as a model and encouragement for other Christian spouses.

38. A further need emphasized by the cardinals and bishops is that of *continental synods,* following the example of those already held for Europe and Africa. The last General Conference of the Latin American Episcopate accepted, in agreement with the bishops of North America, the proposal for *a Synod for the Americas* on the problems of the new evangelization in both parts of the same continent, so different in origin and history, and on issues of justice and of international economic relations, in view of the enormous gap between North and South.

Another plan for a continent-wide synod will concern Asia, where the issue of the encounter of Christianity with ancient local cultures and religions is a pressing one. This is a great challenge for evangelization, since religious systems such as Buddhism or Hinduism have a clearly soteriological character. There is also an urgent need for a synod on the occasion of the Great Jubilee in order to illustrate and explain more fully the truth that Christ is the one Mediator between God and man and the sole Redeemer of the world, to be clearly distinguished from the founders of other great religions. With sincere esteem, the Church regards the elements of truth found in those religions as a reflection of the Truth which enlightens all men and women.[23] *"Ecce natus est nobis Salvator mundi*": In the year 2000 the proclamation of this truth should resound with renewed power.

Also for *Oceania* a regional synod could be useful. In this region there arises the question, among others, of the Aboriginal People, who in a unique way evoke aspects of human prehistory. In this synod a matter not to be overlooked, together with other problems of the region, would be the encounter of Christianity with the most ancient forms of religion, profoundly marked by a monotheistic orientation.

B) SECOND PHASE

39. On the basis of this vast program aimed at creating awareness, it will then be possible to begin the *second phase,* the strictly *preparatory* phase. This will take place *over the span of three years,* from 1997 to 1999. The thematic structure of this three-year period, *centered on Christ,* the Son of God made man, must necessarily be theological, and therefore *Trinitarian.*

YEAR ONE: JESUS CHRIST

40. *The first year,* 1997, will thus be devoted to *reflection on Christ,* the Word of God, made man by the power of the Holy Spirit. *The distinctly Christological character of the Jubilee* needs to be emphasized, for it will celebrate the Incarnation and coming into the world of the Son of God, the mystery of salvation for all mankind. The general theme proposed by many cardinals and bishops for this year is: "Jesus Christ, the one Savior of the world, yesterday, today, and for ever" (cf. Heb 13:8).

Among the Christological themes suggested in the Consistory the following stand out: a renewed appreciation of Christ, Savior and Proclaimer of the Gospel, with special reference to the fourth chapter of the Gospel of Luke, where the theme of Christ's mission of preaching the Good News and the theme of the Jubilee are interwoven; a deeper understanding of the mystery of the Incarnation and of Jesus' birth from the Virgin Mary; the necessity of faith in Christ for salvation. In order to recognize who Christ truly is, Christians, especially in the course of this year, *should turn with renewed interest to the Bible*, "whether it be through the liturgy, rich in the divine Word, or through devotional reading, or through instructions suitable for the purpose and other aids."[24] In the revealed text it is the Heavenly Father Himself who comes to us in love and who dwells with us, disclosing to us the nature of His only-begotten Son and His plan of salvation for humanity.[25]

41. The commitment, mentioned earlier, to make the mystery of salvation sacramentally present can lead, in the course of the year, to a *renewed appreciation of Baptism* as the basis of Christian living, according to the words of the Apostle: "As many of you as were baptized into Christ have put on Christ" (Gal 3:27). The *Catechism of the Catholic Church,* for its part, recalls that Baptism constitutes "the foundation of communion among all Christians, including those who are not yet in full communion with the Catholic Church."[26] From an *ecumenical point of view,* this will certainly be a very important year for Christians to look together to Christ the one Lord, deepening our commitment to become one in Him, in accordance with His prayer to the Father. This emphasis on the centrality of Christ, of the Word of God, and of faith ought to inspire interest among Christians of other denominations and meet with a favorable response from them.

42. Everything ought to focus on the primary objective of the Jubilee: the *strengthening of faith and of the witness of Christians*. It is therefore necessary to inspire in all the faithful *a true longing for holiness*, a deep desire for conversion and personal renewal in a context of ever more intense prayer and of solidarity with one's neighbor, especially the most needy.

The first year therefore will be the opportune moment for a renewed appreciation of *catechesis* in its original meaning as "the Apostles' teaching" (Acts 2:42) about the Person of Jesus Christ and His mystery of salvation. In this regard, a detailed study of the *Catechism of the Catholic Church* will prove of great benefit, for the catechism presents "faithfully and systematically... the teaching of Sacred Scripture, the living Tradition of the Church and the authentic Magisterium, as well as the spiritual heritage of the Fathers, doctors and saints of the Church, to allow for a better knowledge of the Christian mystery and for enlivening the faith of the People of God."[27] To be realistic, we need to enlighten the consciences of the faithful concerning errors regarding the Person of Christ, clarifying objections against Him and against the Church.

43. *The Blessed Virgin*, who will be as it were "indirectly" present in the whole preparatory phase, will be contemplated in this first year especially in the mystery of her divine motherhood. It was in her womb that the Word became flesh! The affirmation of the central place of Christ cannot therefore be separated from the recognition of the role played by his Most Holy Mother. Veneration of her, when properly understood, can in no way take away from "the dignity and efficacy of Christ the one Mediator."[28] Mary in fact constantly points to her Divine Son and she is proposed to all believers as the *model of faith* which is put into practice. "Devotedly meditating on her and contemplating her in the light of the Word made man, the Church with reverence enters more intimately into the supreme mystery of the Incarnation and becomes ever increasingly like her Spouse."[29]

YEAR TWO: THE HOLY SPIRIT

44. 1998, the *second year* of the preparatory phase, will be dedicated in a particular way to the *Holy Spirit* and to His sanctifying presence within the community of Christ's disciples. "The *great Jubilee* at the close of the second millennium...," I wrote in the encyclical *Dominum et Vivificantem*, "has a *pneumatological aspect* since the mystery of the Incarnation was accomplished 'by the power of the Holy Spirit.' It was 'brought about' by that Spirit—consubstantial with the Father and the Son—who, in the absolute mystery of the Triune God, is the Person-love, the uncreated gift, who is the eternal source of every gift that comes from God in the order of creation, the direct principle and, in a certain sense, the subject of God's self-communication in the order of grace. The *mystery of the Incarnation constitutes the climax* of this giving, this divine self-communication."[30]

The Church cannot prepare for the new millennium "in any other way than *in the Holy Spirit.* What was accomplished by the power of the Holy Spirit 'in the fullness of time' can only through the Spirit's power now emerge from the memory of the Church."[31]

The Spirit, in fact, makes present in the Church of every time and place the unique Revelation brought by Christ to humanity, making it alive and active in the soul of each individual: "The Counselor, the Holy Spirit, whom the Father will send in my name, he will teach you all things, and bring to your remembrance all that I have said to you" (Jn 14:26).

45. The primary tasks of the preparation for the Jubilee thus include *a renewed appreciation of the presence and activity of the Spirit,* who acts within the Church both in the sacraments, especially in *Confirmation,* and in the variety of charisms, roles, and ministries which He inspires for the good of the Church: "There is only one Spirit who, according to his own richness and the needs of the ministries, distributes his different gifts for the welfare of the Church (cf. 1 Cor 12:1-11). Among these gifts stands out the grace given to the Apostles. To their authority, the Spirit Himself subjected even those who were endowed with charisms (cf. 1 Cor 14). Giving the body unity through Himself and through His power and through the internal cohesion of its members, this same Spirit produces and urges love among the believers."[32]

In our own day too, the Spirit is *the principal agent of the new evangelization*. Hence it will be important to gain a renewed appreciation of the Spirit as the One who builds the Kingdom of God within the course of history and prepares its full manifestation in Jesus Christ, stirring people's hearts and quickening in our world the seeds of the full salvation which will come at the end of time.

46. In this *eschatological perspective*, believers should be called to a renewed appreciation of the theological virtue *of hope*, which they have already heard proclaimed "in the word of the truth, the Gospel" (Col 1:5). The basic attitude of hope, on the one hand, encourages the Christian not to lose sight of the final goal which gives meaning and value to life, and on the other, offers solid and profound reasons for a daily commitment to transform reality in order to make it correspond to God's plan.

As the Apostle Paul reminds us: "We know that the whole creation has been groaning in travail together until now; and not only the creation, but we ourselves, who have the first fruits of the Spirit, groan inwardly as we wait for adoption as sons, the redemption of our bodies. For in this hope we were saved" (Rom 8:22-24). Christians are called to prepare for the Great Jubilee of the beginning of the third millennium *by renewing their hope in the definitive coming of the Kingdom of God*, preparing for it daily in their hearts, in the Christian community to which they belong, in their particular social context, and in world history itself.

There is also need for a better appreciation and understanding of *the signs of hope present in the last part of this century*, even though they often remain hidden from our eyes. *In society in general*, such signs of hope include: scientific, technological, and especially medical progress in the service of human life, a greater awareness of our responsibility for the environment, efforts to restore peace and justice wherever they have been violated, a desire for reconciliation and solidarity among different peoples, particularly in the complex relationship between the North and the South of the world. *In the Church*, they include a greater attention to the voice of the Spirit through the acceptance of charisms and the promotion of the laity, a deeper commitment to the cause of Christian unity, and the increased interest in dialogue with other religions and with contemporary culture.

47. The reflection of the faithful in the second year of preparation ought to focus particularly *on the value of unity* within the Church, to which the various gifts and charisms bestowed upon her by the Spirit are directed. In this regard, it will be opportune to promote a deeper understanding of the ecclesiological doctrine of the Second Vatican Council as contained primarily in the Dogmatic Constitution *Lumen Gentium*. This important document has expressly emphasized that the unity of the Body of Christ *is founded on the activity of the Spirit*, guaranteed by the apostolic ministry and sustained by mutual love (cf. 1 Cor 13:1-8). This catechetical enrichment of the faith cannot fail to bring the members of the People of God to a more mature awareness of their own responsibilities, as well as to a more lively sense of the importance of ecclesial obedience.[33]

48. *Mary,* who conceived the Incarnate Word by the power of the Holy Spirit and then in the whole of her life allowed herself to be guided by His interior activity, will be contemplated and imitated during this year above all as the woman who was docile to the voice of the Spirit, a woman of silence and attentiveness, a woman of hope who, like Abraham, accepted God's will "hoping against hope" (cf. Rom 4:18). Mary gave full expression to the longing of the poor of Yahweh and is a radiant model for those who entrust themselves with all their hearts to the promises of God.

YEAR THREE: GOD THE FATHER

49. 1999, *the third and final year of preparation,* will be aimed at broadening the horizons of believers so that they will see things in the perspective of Christ: *in the perspective of the "Father who is in heaven"* (cf. Mt 5:45), from whom the Lord was sent and to whom He has returned (cf. Jn 16:28).

"This is eternal life, that they know you the only true God, and Jesus Christ whom you have sent" (cf. Jn 17:3). The whole of the Christian life is like a great *pilgrimage to the house of the Father,* whose unconditional love for every human creature, and in particular for the "prodigal son" (cf. Lk 15:11-32), we discover anew each day. This pilgrimage takes place in the heart of each person, extends to the believing community, and then reaches to the whole of humanity.

The Jubilee, centered on the person of Christ, thus becomes a great act of praise to the Father: "Blessed be the God and Father of our Lord Jesus Christ, who has blessed us in Christ with every spiritual blessing in the heavenly places, even as he chose us in him before the foundation of the world, that we should be holy and blameless before him" (Eph 1:3-4).

50. In this third year the sense of being on a journey to the Father should encourage everyone to undertake, by holding fast to Christ the Redeemer of man, a journey of authentic *conversion*. This includes both a "negative" aspect, that of liberation from sin, and a "positive" aspect, that of choosing good, accepting the ethical values expressed in the natural law, which is confirmed and deepened by the Gospel. This is the proper context for a renewed appreciation and more intense celebration of the *Sacrament of Penance* in its most profound meaning. The call to conversion as the indispensable condition of Christian love is particularly important in contemporary society, where the very foundations of an ethically correct vision of human existence often seem to have been lost.

It will therefore be necessary, especially during this year, to emphasize the theological virtue of *charity*, recalling the significant and lapidary words of the First Letter of John: "God is love" (4:8, 16). Charity, in its twofold reality as love of God and neighbor, is the summing up of the moral life of the believer. It has in God its source and its goal.

51. From this point of view, if we recall that Jesus came to "preach the good news to the poor" (cf. Mt 11:5; Lk 7:22), how can we fail to lay greater emphasis on the *Church's preferential option for the poor and the outcast?* Indeed,it has to be said that a commitment to justice and peace in a world like ours, marked by so many conflicts and intolerable social and economic inequalities, is a necessary condition for the preparation and celebration of the Jubilee. Thus, in the spirit of the Book of Leviticus (25:8-12), Christians will have to raise their voice on behalf of all the poor of the world, proposing the Jubilee as an appropriate time to give thought, among other things, to reducing substantially, if not canceling outright, the international debt which seriously threatens the future of many nations. The Jubilee can also offer an opportunity for reflecting on other challenges of our time, such as the difficulties of dialogue between different cultures and the problems connected with respect for women's rights and the promotion of the family and marriage.

52. Recalling that "Christ,... by the revelation of the mystery of the Father and his love, fully reveals man to man himself and makes his supreme calling clear,"[34] two commitments should characterize in a special way the third preparatory year: *meeting the challenge of secularism and dialogue with the great religions.*

With regard to the former, it will be fitting to broach the vast subject of the *crisis of civilization,* which has become apparent especially in the West, which is highly developed from the standpoint of technology but is interiorly impoverished by its tendency to forget God or to keep Him at a distance. This crisis of civilization must be countered by *the civilization of love,* founded on the universal values of peace, solidarity, justice, and liberty, which find their full attainment in Christ.

53. On the other hand, as far as the field of religious awareness is concerned, the eve of the year 2000 will provide a great opportunity, especially in view of the events of recent decades, for *interreligious dialogue,* in accordance with the specific guidelines set down by the Second Vatican Council in its declaration *Nostra Aetate* on the relationship of the Church to non-Christian religions.

In this dialogue the Jews and the Muslims ought to have a preeminent place. God grant that as a confirmation of these intentions it may also be possible to hold *joint meetings* in places of significance for the great monotheistic religions.

In this regard, attention is being given to finding ways of arranging historic meetings in places of exceptional symbolic importance like Bethlehem, Jerusalem, and Mount Sinai as a means of furthering dialogue with Jews and the followers of Islam, and to arranging similar meetings elsewhere with the leaders of the great world religions. However, care will always have [to] be taken not to cause harmful misunderstandings, avoiding the risk of syncretism and of a facile and deceptive irenicism.

54. In this broad perspective of commitments, *Mary Most Holy,* the highly favored daughter of the Father, will appear before the eyes of believers as the perfect model of love toward both God and neighbor. As she herself says in the canticle of the *Magnificat*, great things were done for her by the Almighty, whose name is holy (cf. Lk 1:49). The Father chose her for a *unique mission* in the history of salvation: that of being the Mother of the long-awaited Savior. The Virgin Mary responded to God's call with complete openness: "Behold, I am the handmaid of the Lord" (Lk 1:38). Her motherhood, which began in Nazareth and was lived most intensely in Jerusalem at the foot of the Cross, will be felt during this year as a loving and urgent invitation addressed to all the children of God so that they will return to the house of the Father when they hear her maternal voice: "Do whatever Christ tells you" (cf. Jn 2:5).

C) Approaching the Celebration

55. A separate chapter will be the *actual celebration of the Great Jubilee,* which will take place simultaneously in the Holy Land, in Rome, and in the local churches throughout the world. Especially in this phase, the *phase of celebration,* the aim will be *to give glory to the Trinity,* from whom everything in the world and in history comes and to whom everything returns. This mystery is the focus of the three years of immediate preparation: from Christ and through Christ, in the Holy Spirit, to the Father. In this sense the Jubilee celebration makes present in an anticipatory way the goal and fulfillment of the life of each Christian and of the whole Church in the Triune God.

But since Christ is the only way to the Father, in order to highlight His living and saving presence in the Church and the world, the *International Eucharistic Congress* will take place in Rome, on the occasion of the Great Jubilee. The year 2000 will be intensely eucharistic: in the *Sacrament of the Eucharist* the Savior, who took flesh in Mary's womb twenty centuries ago, continues to offer Himself to humanity as the source of divine life.

The ecumenical and universal character of the sacred Jubilee can be fittingly reflected by a *meeting of all Christians.* This would be an event of great significance, and so, in order to avoid misunderstandings, it should be properly presented and carefully prepared, in an attitude of fraternal cooperation with Christians of other denominations and traditions, as well as of grateful openness to those religions whose representatives might wish to acknowledge the joy shared by all the disciples of Christ.

One thing is certain: Everyone is asked to do as much as possible to ensure that the great challenge of the year 2000 is not overlooked, for this challenge certainly involves a special grace of the Lord for the Church and for the whole of humanity.

V
CONCLUSION

56. The Church has endured for two thousand years. Like the *mustard seed* in the Gospel, she has grown and become a great tree, able to cover the whole of humanity with her branches (cf. Mt 13:31-32). The Second Vatican Council, in its Dogmatic Constitution on the Church, thus addresses the question of *membership in the Church and the call of all people*

to belong to the People of God: "All are called to be part of this Catholic unity of the new People of God....
And there belong to it or are related to it in various ways the Catholic faithful as well as all who believe in Christ, and indeed the whole of mankind, which by the grace of God is called to salvation."[35] Pope Paul VI, in the encyclical *Ecclesiam Suam,* illustrates how all mankind is involved in the plan of God and emphasizes the various circles of the dialogue of salvation.[36]

Continuing this approach, we can also appreciate more clearly the Gospel parable of the leaven (cf. Mt 13:33): Christ, like a divine leaven, always and ever more fully penetrates the life of humanity, spreading the work of salvation accomplished in the Paschal Mystery. What is more, He embraces within His redemptive power *the whole past history* of the human race, beginning with the first Adam.[37] The *future* also belongs to Him: "Jesus Christ is the same yesterday and today and for ever" (Heb 13:8). For her part the Church "seeks but a solitary goal: to carry forward the work of Christ himself under the lead of the Holy Spirit, the Paraclete. And Christ entered this world to give witness to the truth, to rescue and not to sit in judgment, to serve and not to be served."[38]

57. Therefore, ever since the apostolic age *the Church's mission* has continued without interruption within the whole human family. The first evangelization took place above all in the region of the Mediterranean. In the course of the first millennium, missions setting out from Rome and Constantinople brought Christianity to *the whole continent of Europe.* At the same time they made their way to the heart of *Asia,* as far as India and China. The end of the fifteenth century marked both the discovery of *America* and the beginning of the evangelization of those great continents, North and South. Simultaneously, while the sub-Saharan coasts of Africa welcomed the light of Christ, St. Francis Xavier, Patron of the Missions, reached Japan. At the end of the eighteenth century and the beginning of the nineteenth, a layman, Andrew Kim, brought Christianity to Korea. In the same period the proclamation of the Gospel reached Indochina, as well as *Australia and the islands of the Pacific.*

The nineteenth century witnessed vast missionary activity among the *peoples of Africa.* All these efforts bore fruit which has lasted up to the present day. The Second Vatican Council gives an account of this in the decree *Ad Gentes* on Missionary Activity. After the Council the question of missionary work was dealt with in the encyclical *Redemptoris Missio,* in the light of the problems of the missions in these final years of our century. In the future, too, the Church must continue to be missionary: Indeed missionary outreach is part of her very nature. With the fall of the great anti-Christian systems in Europe, first of Nazism and then of Communism, there is urgent need to bring once more the liberating message of the Gospel to the men and women of Europe.[39] Furthermore, as the encyclical *Redemptoris Missio* affirms, the modern world reflects the situation of the *Areopagus of Athens,* where St. Paul spoke.[40] Today there are many "*areopagi,*" and very different ones: These are the vast sectors of contemporary civilization and culture, of politics and economics. *The more the West is becoming estranged from its Christian roots, the more it is becoming missionary territory,* taking the form of many different *"areopagi."*

58. The future of the world and the Church belongs to the *younger generation,* to those who born in this century will reach maturity in the next, the first century of the new millennium. *Christ expects great things from young people,* as He did from the young man who asked Him: "What good deed must I do, to have eternal life?" (Mt 19:16). I have referred to the remarkable answer which Jesus gave to him in the recent encyclical *Veritatis Splendor,* as I did earlier, in 1985, in my *Apostolic Letter to the Youth of the World.* Young people, in every situation, in every region of the world, do not cease to put questions to Christ: *They meet Him and they keep searching for Him in order to question Him further.* If they succeed in following the road which He points out to them, they will have the joy of making their own contribution to His presence in the next century and in the centuries to come, until the end of time: "Jesus is the same yesterday, today, and for ever."

59. In conclusion, it is helpful to recall the words of the Pastoral Constitution *Gaudium et Spes:* "The Church believes that Christ, who died and was raised up for all, can through his Spirit offer man the light and the strength to measure up to his supreme destiny. Nor has any other name under heaven been given to man by which it is fitting for him to be saved. She likewise holds that *in her most benign Lord and Master can be found the key, the focal point and the* *goal of all human history.* The Church also maintains that beneath all changes there are *so many realities which do not change and which have their ultimate founda-tion in Christ,* who is the same yesterday and today and forever. Hence in the light of Christ, the image of the unseen God, the firstborn of every creature, the Council wishes to speak to all men in order to illuminate the mystery of man and to cooperate in finding the solution to the outstanding problems of our time."[41]

While I invite the faithful to raise to the Lord fervent prayers to obtain the light and assistance necessary for the preparation and celebration of the forthcoming Jubilee, I exhort my venerable brothers in the Episcopate and the ecclesial communities entrusted to them to open their hearts to the promptings of the Spirit. He will not fail to arouse enthusiasm and lead people to celebrate the Jubilee with renewed faith and generous participation.

I entrust this responsibility of the whole Church to the maternal intercession of Mary, Mother of the Redeemer. She, the Mother of Fairest Love, will be for Christians on the way to the Great Jubilee of the third millennium the star which safely guides their steps to the Lord. May the unassuming young woman of Nazareth, who two thousand years ago offered to the world the Incarnate Word, lead the men and women of the new millennium toward the One who is "the true light that enlightens every man" (Jn 1:9).

With these sentiments I impart to all my Blessing.

From the Vatican, on 10 November in the year 1994, the seventeenth of my pontificate.

NOTES

1998
YEAR TWO OF PREPARATION
Focusing on God the Holy Spirit

1. *Roman Missal,* Sequence for Easter Sunday.
2. *Lumen Gentium,* 68.
3. See St. Augustine, *De Civitate Dei,* XXII, 17: CCL48, 835f; St. Thomas Aquinas, *Summa Theologiae,* III pars., q. 64, art. 2 *ad tertium.*
4. *Lumen Gentium,* 39.
5. *Lumen Gentium,* 4.
6. John Paul II, The Apostolic Exhortation on the Family *Familiaris Consortio,* 33.
7. *Lumen Gentium,* 5.
8. *Lumen Gentium,* 5.
9. *Lumen Gaudium,* 28.
10. John Paul II, Apostolic Exhortation *Catechesi Tradendae,* 67: *AAS* 71 (1979), 1333.
11. Code of Canon Law, Can. 515,S 1.
12. *Lumen Gentium,* 15.
13. John Paul II, Homily at the Solemn Eucharistic Con-celebration for the Close of the Seventh Ordinary General Assembly of the Synod of Bishops (October 30, 1987): *AAS* 80 (1988), 600.
14. *Lumen Gentium,* 37.
15. *Lumen Gentium,* 35.
16. *Lumen Gentium,* 12.
17. *Lumen Gentium,* 35.

1. Cf. Saint Bernard, *In Laudibus Virginis Matris, Homilia IV*, 8, *Opera Omnia*, Edit. Cister. (1966), 53.
2. *Gaudium et Spes*, 22.
3. *Gaudium et Spes*, 22.
4. Cf. *Ant. Iud.* 20:200, and the well-known and much-discussed passage in 18:63-64.
5. *Annales* 15:44, 3.
6. *Vita Claudii*, 25:4.
7. *Epist.* 10:96.
8. *Dei Verbum*, 15.
9. Encyclical Letter *Redemptor Hominis* (4 March 1979), 1: *AAS* 71 (1979), 258.
10. Cf. Encyclical Letter *Dominum et Vivificantem* (18 May 1986), 49ff.: *AAS* 79 (1986), 868ff.
11. Cf. Apostolic Letter *Euntes in Mundum* (25 January 1988): *AAS* 80 (1988), 935-56.
12. Cf. Encyclical Letter *Centesimus Annus* (1 May 1991), 12: *AAS* 83 (1991), 807-809.
13. *Gaudium et Spes*, 47-52.
14. *Lumen Gentium*, 1.
15. Cf. Apostolic Exhortation *Reconciliatio et Paenitentia* (2 December 1984): AAS 77 (1985), 185-275.
16. *Lumen Gentium*, 8.
17. *Unitatis Redintegratio*, 3.
18. *Unitatis Redintegratio*, 1.
19. Vatican II, Declaration on Religious Freedom *Dignitatis Humanae*, 1.
20. *Gaudium et Spes*, 19.
21. Tertullian, *Apol.*, 50:13: *CCL* 1:171.
22. Cf. *AAS* 56 (1964), 906.
23. *Nostra Aetate*, 2.
24. *Dei Verbum*, 25.
25. *Dei Verbum*, 2.
26. *Catechism of the Catholic Church*, No. 1271.
27. Apostolic Constitution *Fidei Depositum* (11 October 1992).
28. *Lumen Gentium*, 62.
29. *Lumen Gentium*, 65.

30. Encyclical Letter *Dominum et Vivificantem* (18 May 1986), 50: *AAS* 78 (1986), 869-870.
31. *Dominum et Vivificantem*, 51: *AAS* 78 (1986), 871.
32. *Lumen Gentium*, 7.
33. *Lumen Gentium*, 37.
34. *Gaudium et Spes*, 22.
35. *Lumen Gentium*, 13.
36. Cf. Paul VI, Encyclical Letter *Ecclesiam Suam* (6 August 1964), III: *AAS* 56 (1964), 650-657.
37. *Ecclesiam Suam*, 2.
38. *Gaudium et Spes*, 3.
39. Cf. Declaration of the Special Assembly for Europe of the Synod of Bishops, No. 3.
40. Cf. Encyclical *Redemptoris Missio* (7 December 1990), 37:AAS 83 (1991), 284-286.
41. *Gaudium et Spes*, 10.

*Other Books of Interest
in the Celebrate 2000! Series*

Celebrate 2000! A Three Year Reader
POPE JOHN PAUL II

This handsome hardback volume contains weekly readings on God the Father, Son, and Holy Spirit compiled from the inspirations writings of the Holy Father. $17.99

Rekindle Your Love for Jesus
DAVID E. ROSAGE

In this book the bestselling author of *Speak, Lord, Your Servant Is Listening* leads readers to a fuller, more vital understanding of what it means to follow Jesus in daily life. $9.99

Mary, Star of the New Millennium
DAVID E. ROSAGE

This book explores the important and powerful role Mary plays in these days of "Great Renewal." Monsignor Rosage shows readers how Mary is like a guiding star who points our way to God. $10.99

Refresh Your Life in the Spirit
BABSIE BLEASDELL WITH HENRY LIBERSAT

A lively and very personal testimony of how the Holy Spirit can transform your life and help you tap into the spiritual gifts all believers have been given through Baptism. $10.99

Available at your local Christian bookstore, or from

Servant Publications, PO Box 8617, Ann Arbor, MI 48107-8617
Please include payment plus $3.25 per book for shipping and handling.